Economics of Sustainable Development

Economics of Sustainable Development

Runa Sarkar and Anup Sinha

BEP BUSINESS EXPERT PRESS

Economics of Sustainable Development

First published in 2018 by
Business Expert Press, LLC
222 East 46th Street, New York, NY 10017
www.businessexpertpress.com

ISBN-13: 978-1-63157-104-6 (paperback)
ISBN-13: 978-1-63157-105-3 (e-book)

Business Expert Press Economics Collection

Collection ISSN: 2163-761X (print)
Collection ISSN: 2163-7628 (electronic)

Cover and interior design by Exeter Premedia Services Private Ltd., Chennai, India

First edition: 2018

10 9 8 7 6 5 4 3 2 1

Printed in the United States of America.

Abstract

This book analyses the concept of sustainable development from the perspective of economics. The concept of sustainability has become an integral part of business strategies across the world. Regulations that govern business have changed in order to facilitate sustainable processes, as have consumer preferences in demanding more environmentally clean products. The perceived importance of being green, whether in company board rooms or in government policy-making circles, is not always backed up by an adequate understanding of the complexities of the concept, and their implications for decision-making.

It is important to have an understanding of these complexities and the economic logic underlying both the necessity and the difficulty of moving to a world that can be sustained over time. At the core of the concept of sustainable development lies the inter-relationship between the activities of human societies and nature. An understanding of this inter-relationship goes beyond the domain of conventional economics, into more interfaced terrains of ecological economics and environmental science.

This book attempts to sensitize the business practitioner and the public-policy planner, as well as students of business management and the social sciences, to the complexities of the concept of sustainable development in an easily comprehensible manner. Without an appreciation of the different aspects and dimensions of sustainability, policy and practice often tend to come up with mutually inconsistent strategies that do not add up to the dynamic goal of sustainable development for future residents of planet earth.

Keywords

carrying capacity, climate change, collective action, ecological footprint, economic development, economic growth, ecosystem services, ecosystems, environment, genuine investment, global governance, inter-generational well-being, international political economy, intra-generational well-being, market failures, social discount rate, sustainable development, time preference, weak and strong sustainable development

Contents

CHAPTER 1

The Meaning of Economic Development

Sustainable development is a recent addition to the lexicon of terms used in understanding the problems of economic development and growth. The term has attained the status of a *buzzword*, with everyone using it, often without a clear understanding of its implications. One hears about sustainable growth, sustainable business, sustainable consumption and production, and of course, sustainable development. There are a number of different views on the matter and the term is fraught with imprecisions, complexities, and ethical ambiguities (Pezzey and Toman 2002). The alternative origins of the meaning of sustainable development come from religious texts; modern scientific knowledge, such as atmospheric physics, environmental science, and evolutionary biology; social sciences, including sociology, economics, anthropology, political science, history and even literature. Philosophers too have contributed to the development of the concept.

However, there is one important aspect of sustainable development that is common to all the different points of view. This common point lies in the need to develop a deeper understanding of the relationship of human beings and their activities with the natural environment over time. This implies that the human–nature relationship is something that transcends geographical, political, or cultural particularities. Nature is also shared by all living beings, including humans. Therefore, any process of change that is sustainable over time has to be necessarily global in character. For instance, if an economically developed country, say Sweden, uses natural resources in a sustainable fashion, it may not be a solution for the whole world (or even Sweden itself) if other nations and other communities do not follow suit.

This book is about the economics of sustainable development. While the focus of the book, therefore, will be on the economic aspects, it will draw from other disciplines from time to time. The study of economics, as a means of understanding the extent of human welfare, has existed for over centuries. The concept of economic development is a relatively newer construct that began to emerge, as the industrial revolution created the possibility of unbridled progress and hitherto unheard of improvements in human wellbeing. These changes began with the transition from feudalism to capitalism in Western Europe. This process of consistent and rapid economic growth became the centerpiece of the study of economic development. Questions around economic growth, such as what were the social and institutional parameters needed to sustain it, what were the critical resources necessary, and the role of new technology comprised the modern study of economic development.

The common persons' perception of economic development is also strongly rooted in improvements in material living, attained by higher incomes earned. Higher incomes help the person consume more goods and services, as well as save for an uncertain future. Economists and policymakers use this as a guideline to measure economic development of an entire community or nation of people. Though the level of income and the rate of growth of national income continue to remain the two most commonly used metrics of economic development, economists also acknowledge that there is more to development than just overall growth. The importance of other aspects of development, such as having access to opportunities for education, good health services, sufficient resources so as to maintain a reasonable quality of life, all have led to the use of new indices such as the human development index (HDI) to characterize economic development. This perception of continuous economic growth and material improvement in daily living was not always the dominant idea among economists. It is to this discussion that we now turn.

A Brief History of the Discourse of Economic Development

The Classical School

The school of classical economics represented by pioneers in modern economic theory, such as Adam Smith, David Ricardo, Thomas Malthus, and John Stuart Mill, had a more complex view of economic development.

To all of them, economic development did lead to the greater production of goods and services, but its success was contingent on a large number of interacting factors. To start with, the emphasis was on the *wealth of nations*, that is, the stock of productive capital necessary to generate growth in the flow of national income. In order to accumulate such productive capital, there had to be an efficient division of labor and resources so as to maximize productivity, which, in turn, would generate a surplus for investments and accumulation of capital. Specialization was not restricted to the division of labor, but also extended to economies as a whole, as exemplified by the notion of comparative advantage and the benefits of international trade. The entire economy would require the generation of a surplus over and above the consumption requirements of society. This surplus (or profits) was considered the key to new investments and the accumulation of the capital stock. Thus, economic development was viewed as a dynamic process driven by the generation of profits earned by enterprises competing in different markets. These markets would have to be governed by the state in terms of appropriate rules and laws. These economists recognized the importance of social regulation of economic activities. Despite Adam Smith's name being associated with the benefits of the *invisible hand* of the markets in the allocation of resources, he also spoke of the need for good governance to ensure the smooth functioning of markets.

The classical economists shared a common concern about the nature of land and agricultural activities in the context of rapid industrialization across the world. They realized that industrial capital in the form of machinery and factories could be built and rebuilt repeatedly (reproduced) with very little requirement of land, unlike in agriculture. There were an increasing number of workers who would be moving from agriculture to industry who needed to be fed from the produce of the agricultural sector, although they contributed nothing to the production of food. Agricultural land was fixed in quantity, and human beings could not accumulate it. When all the available land, including the relatively infertile land, had been used up, agricultural land would pose a limiting constraint on maintaining a rising industrial population. Hence, all of these economists considered land as the constraint that would pull down industrial growth to zero. They all had some vision either of a stationary state, or some periodic crisis, that would correct the imbalance between food supply and demand.

For Smith, the emphasis was to keep international trade going so that the advent of the stationary state in any one economy could be postponed till all available land worldwide had been fully utilized (Smith 1776/1976). Ricardo was of a similar opinion and demonstrated that the return to land (the rent earned by landlords) emerged from its scarcity value in terms of productivity (Ricardo 1966). Once the least productive (marginal) land was utilized, there would be no rent left. In any case, according to Ricardo, the rent earned by landlords would not be used for productive investment because landowners were different from industrial capitalists and were not interested in the accumulation of productive capital. Malthus argued that, instead of a stationary state, there would be periodic imbalances in the availability of food, growing linearly, and its geometrically increasing demand from a growing population in the industrial sector (Malthus 1826). These imbalances would self-correct, but only at a large social cost of famine, pestilence, or war. An alternative conception of the stationary state was provided by John Stuart Mill, who argued that societies would realize the implications of an impending stationary state and might choose to limit material growth and focus on improving the quality of life, which he referred to as culture and *social graces* (Mill 1909). All these economists shared a common concern about the limits to growth of industry because of the constraint of a fixed quantity of land as a natural resource.

The Optimism of the Industrial Revolution

The rapid expansion of industrialization in Western Europe along with its far-reaching impacts on the economies of Asia, Africa, and the Americas shifted the attention of economists from the study of production and distribution of goods and services within an economy to a deeper understanding of market mechanisms and the determination of prices. By the late 19th century, economists in Europe analyzed economic activities at a point of time without explicitly focusing on its dynamics (Walras 2013/1874; Marshall 1920). They assumed that the total resources of an economy were fixed at a given moment of time. The analytical challenge, then, was to explain how, given these resources, the market mechanism through the signaling role of prices optimally allocated the scarce (fixed) resources among alternative productive uses. Production, in turn, would be determined by the preferences of consumers signaled by their demand. The methodology was one of possessive individualism, where an individual or business firm was endowed with some income or resources to start with. The consumer would translate his or her income into an optimal basket of goods that would maximize his or her satisfaction from consumption. The business firm, on the other hand, would determine the quantity of inputs and their appropriate combination for producing goods and services at least cost. Decisions were taken on the basis of small incremental (marginal) changes on the net benefit for producers and consumers. Hence, it centered on achieving optimal solutions, that is, the best solution available under a given set of economic constraints such as income, resources and prices. This method would obviously focus on attaining local (in a mathematical sense) solutions[1] for the efficient allocation of scarce resources, be it income for the consumer or inputs for the producer. Under perfect conditions of well-functioning markets, this method of decision-making would lead to the full utilization of all available productive resources in the most efficient manner. If prices were completely flexible, any unused resource would lead to a fall in that price, which, in turn, would induce a greater demand for the resource, till the point where the market *cleared*, that is, the demand for the resource exactly matched its availability. Thus, markets and the price mechanism would play a key role in ensuring that marginal returns were equated to marginal costs in all economic activities. The net outcome was that, all available resources in an economy would be fully and efficiently utilized. The analytical focus shifted from the society and economy changing over time to individual consumers and producers allocating resources at a moment of time.

This approach did not address the question of the size of the total availability of resources and whether it was increasing or shrinking. Nor was any explanation provided as to where the initial endowments

---

[1] It means that, if a mathematical solution is perturbed by a very tiny amount, how would the solution change? Large changes in the variables are ruled out.

of resources came from. Hence, there were no questions either about overall economic growth or the limits to growth. It is interesting to note that the fixity of economy-wide resources did not distinguish about any special feature of land as a natural resource, or the presence of any exhaustible resource such as forests or fossil fuels. All productive inputs were assumed to be substitutable with one another within certain bounds. This shift in the treatment of productive resources was because of the growing importance of industry *vis-a-vis* agriculture with the former being much more dependent on physical capital (reproducible machinery) than the latter that depended heavily on natural resources. During this time, the possibility of enhancing the productivity of a natural resource such as land was eminently possible with the use of industrially produced inputs like agricultural machinery, fertilizers, and pesticides. Given the way the world was changing, a belief began to emerge that science-based technological improvements could lead to increased productivity of a given resource, without significantly affecting its total availability.

The Great Depression and its Aftermath

By the 1920s, the dominant wisdom in economics was that markets and the price mechanism would *always* lead to the efficient (best-use) and full employment of all resources. This wisdom received a big jolt with the Great Depression of the 1930s, which led to the large-scale unemployment of labor and capital. It spread throughout the market economies of the world, with the worst impact being experienced in the most industrialized economies. The experience of the Great Depression brought into focus the essential role of the state in managing the economy. John Maynard Keynes influenced a whole generation of economists by pointing out that markets, left to their own devices, could not guarantee the full employment of resources (Keynes 1936). The role of the state would have to go beyond the mere provision of national defense, law and order, and the protection of property rights. Hence, economic policy would be one of active intervention in the economy to ensure the smooth functioning of the market system. This was a significant departure from *laissez faire* and free markets.

The decade of the 1930s also witnessed two other major changes that influenced mainstream economic thinking to a large extent. Economists like Robinson (1933) and Chamberlin (1933) argued that markets, particularly for manufactured industrial goods, were hardly perfect in terms of the degree of competition and the determination of prices. A new theory of imperfect competition (the study of monopolies, monopolistic competition, and various forms of oligopolies) emerged. Under imperfect conditions of competition, the price mechanism did not lead to the best allocation of resources for society. Producers could have a direct role in price setting, which would normally be higher than the incremental cost in the making of the good. Perfect markets and the best allocation of resources came to be contested in a very fundamental way.

The other influential change that left a long-lasting impact on the economic theory was due to the work of the famous economist Roy Harrod, who no longer accepted the fixity of productive resources in an economy (Harrod 1939). Indeed, he argued that resources could be increased indefinitely through the process of capital accumulation and economic growth. He resurrected the concept of profits being ploughed back to create more capital stock that the classical economists had portrayed, but with a difference. In Harrod's conception, no resource (land or any other) provided a limiting constraint on the process of accumulation. As long as an economy had a surplus (saving) over current consumption, it could be invested in creating and producing more capital stock, which would enhance the total productive capacity of the economy over time. This could (under certain circumstances) result in an indefinite growth of an economy, described as a steady state. Later, economists like Robert Solow refined the idea of the steady state with population growth and technological progress (Solow 1956). Hence, from the individual concerns for optimal solutions of microeconomics, a new aspect of the economy theory (macroeconomics) looked at the possibility of indefinite compound economic growth. This possibility would be realized through markets, and if necessary, by an astute intervention of the policymakers of the economy.

Economists in the 1940s and 1950s looked not only at the role of government in stabilizing markets through suitable monetary and fiscal policies, but also its role as an agent of industrialization. In the post-world war era of reconstruction, and the emergence of newly independent former colonies, many economists came up with new theories of economic development. Growth of GDP[2] was disaggregated into sectoral investments and structural change. For instance, Rostow (1960) came up with his well-known stages of economic growth, which described how an economy transformed itself from a low-income-low-saving-low-growth to a high-income-high-investment-high-growth economy. Some of the other theories focused on the sectoral balance in investment and growth (Nurkse 1961, Rosenstien-Rodan 1943), while others like Hirschman (1969) talked about an industrial strategy of promoting a leading sector with maximum linkage effects with the rest of the economy, a process described as unbalanced growth. Around the same time, Arthur Lewis's famous paper (1954) analyzed how the presence of even a small industrial modern sector could transform a labor-surplus traditional economy into a market-driven one, with high rates of capital accumulation. During this period, economists accepted the private sector, as well as the public sector, or government as distinct sources of productive investment flows. For some economists, the role of the state was quite essential in creating a *big push* for investments—referred to as the critical minimum effort (Nelson 1956). Hence, by the 1960s and 1970s, both mature market economies and less developed or emerging market economies, influenced by the conventional wisdom of the times, accepted a crucial role for the state in policy intervention for fiscal, monetary, as well as industrialization strategies. However, by the 1970s and 1980s, despite active role of governments in promoting development through industrialization, such as in the newly independent former colonies, poverty, unemployment, and basic material deprivation was rampant and simply refused to go away with macroeconomic growth. Economists drew upon the tradition of welfare economics to look at the process of development beyond industrialization and growth of GDP. Serious questions of how to reduce poverty and address issues related to food security and employment opportunity began to be raised. These questions led to the development of analysis that focused on social outcomes, rather than mere quantitative economic growth.

---

[2] Gross domestic product is a measure of the value of a nation's production of new goods and services in a period of time (usually a year).

The Advent of Welfare Economics

The tradition of going beyond the merely quantitative was not entirely new to the field of economics. Many decades ago, philosophers like Bentham (1907) had defined a good social outcome as one where the level of utility (a subjective state of wellbeing) of every individual was the highest. This outcome, in turn, would imply that the sum total of utility (or satisfaction) in society would also be the highest. This idea of utility as a philosophical concept had a great appeal for economists in assessing economic outcomes. Pigou (1964) restricted the concept of utility to pure economic terms, measurable in terms of a monetary yardstick. Hence, economic utility would be determined by the happiness caused by the use of purchased goods and services. Utility could be linked to economic growth in this sense—higher amount of goods and services produced would be able to create a higher level of utility. This concept of utility later became the cornerstone of the notion of economic welfare both at the individual and the social level. Much earlier, Pareto (1971/1906) had propounded a criterion of comparing social outcomes. According to him, the social outcome (say A) is superior to another social outcome (say B), if in A, at least one person was better off than in B and no person was worse off. Each individual state of affairs was now easily measurable by the state of utility. A Pareto superior outcome, therefore, implied that social utility was higher than before. Pigou was aware that, in a market economy, the distribution of income and wealth might become too unequal. In such a situation, if economic welfare was to be measured by utility, then taking one unit of income from the rich with low marginal utility and giving it to a poor person with high marginal utility of income would result in a higher total utility for society.

This idea has been used in many later economic formulations, such as the compensation principle. Economists such as Hicks (1939) and Kaldor (1939) pointed out that many effects of economic policy would obviously have direct beneficiaries, as well as people adversely affected by the policy. For instance, in a tax-subsidy situation, the direct beneficiary is the one who gets the subsidy, while the tax payer is worse off. They argued that the policy would be acceptable if the losers could be compensated by the winners through a suitable redistributive mechanism, and yet remain better off after the redistribution. A question remained, however, regarding the possibility of comparing utilities across individuals, and hence, the importance of the Pareto criteria remained. Another line of development in welfare economics came from the concepts developed by Bergson (1938), formalized by Samuelson (1956), of the social welfare function. This mathematical function was a representation of social welfare with arguments like individual utilities, goods produced, goods consumed, and resources used up in the process. Unlike GDP, this concept of welfare or *goodness* of a state of affairs involved value judgments and ethical choices made by individuals. This represented a complete swing from a purely objective metric to an entirely normative one. The difficulties of using the social welfare function was highlighted by the famous Arrow impossibility theorem (Arrow 1963), which demonstrated that finding a function exhibiting a minimal set of desired properties such as non-dictatorship (where the social preference coincides with the preference of an individual against all other individuals)was impossible. This made choosing a social state of affairs that was most desirable based on an acceptable welfare function well-nigh impossible.

Later, economists like Sen (1984, 2002) who were concerned about issues like poverty and inequality heavily critiqued utilitarianism as an adequate tool to understand and evaluate economic outcomes. Sen emphasized the agency aspect of human beings in terms of their capabilities, that is, their abilities to do certain things to be as important as subjective levels of satisfaction. Sen developed a theory of capabilities based on rights and entitlements as a measure of economic development. He considered development to be the increasing freedom to acquire the capabilities to do and achieve certain valuable functionings by individuals. This process was not dependent on markets in any fundamental way, but rather on the role of institutions and entitlements in general.

Thus, what we see are two interrelated strands of thinking emerging from the aforementioned discussion. One focuses on economic development as a macroeconomic phenomenon with issues related to GDP growth, distribution of wealth, stability of markets, investments and capital accumulation, role of international trade, and role of the state. This is about the transformation of the economy from an agrarian one to being dominated by industrial production and modern services.

The other strand focuses on development as improvements in the individual's wellbeing, that is, changes affecting the individual's life and work. This relates to issues such as adequate income, access to an increasing set of economic opportunities, economic security, basic capabilities such as health and education, and having a voice in society. It also addresses the rights and freedoms available to individuals, as well as to the inevitability of making ethical judgments when evaluating alternative states of affairs. Starting from the individual and moving to economy-wide outcomes obviously is a more complex process and involves problems of measurement and normative judgments where a plurality of outcomes is inevitable.

The Heterodox School

The aforementioned discussion attempts to identify the threads of arguments and analysis that have contributed to the making of the conventional or mainstream wisdom of economic development. Alongside this tradition, there has also been a heterodox line of thinking about economic development as the progression of social dynamics and the interplay of institutions, technologies, social and economic systems, and politics. One might argue that Marx (1981) has been the single most influential thinker in this tradition. Marx's idea of human beings differed from mainstream thinkers in a fundamental way. According to Marx, the *homoeconomicus* was the creation of the capitalist order of things, with its emphasis on material consumption and its purely hedonistic philosophy of wellbeing. Marx argued that human beings were essentially creative in nature and consumption was much less important than the urge to make things and understand the physical environment of the world. This indeed was supposed to be the *differentia specifica* between humans as a species being and other forms of life. Marx's view of history was dynamic. According to him, in its prehistory, human beings lived in an undifferentiated unity with nature. That was possibly the initial hunter-gatherer stage of human history. Then, as human beings tried to understand the environment and influence it to their own advantage, a second stage of human history could be discerned. This was a stage that reached a height during the renaissance and the enlightenment when human beings were completely alienated from nature. Nature was considered to be outside of human society, something to be controlled and utilized to benefit human beings. This was the age of science and technology when nature became equivalent to other *things* rather than being a part of human life on the planet. In trying to understand and control nature, knowledge of the world increased manifold, as did human beings' knowledge about themselves. This led to the development of the human sciences like biology, medicine, psychology, as well as social sciences such as economics and philosophy. Marx did not stop here. In his view, this stage of alienation was untenable because human beings were a part of nature. It represented only a particular phase of human history. Hence, he argued that there would be a return to nature as our understanding of the environment became more sophisticated. However, this return to nature would be more differentiated and nuanced as compared to the past. The harmony with nature would be re-established, but in terms of a more complex, evolving relationship.

In the backdrop of this philosophy, Marx (1959/1844) argued that capitalism was but one chapter of human history. It emerged out of the feudalism in Europe and would be replaced by an improved social order, which he called socialism or communism. The capitalist economy (market-driven industrialized economy) had a huge positive side in terms of the creation and use of science-based technology, which made the productivity of labor and other resources exceedingly high, without actually needing a large quantity of land. In this sense, Marx was different from his contemporaries who had argued about a stationary state. For Marx, the possibility of technological progress, which would raise the productivity of labor, was inexorable. However, on the negative side, Marx argued that capitalism, with its dependence on private property, appropriated the means of production (resources like productive capital and land) and created a class of people (the working class) who did not own the means of production and could only sell their ability to work (labor power) in the market. The worth of what the workers actually produced was much more than the value the product commanded in the market with the surplus accruing to the owners of the means of production. This, according to Marx, was exploitative and unfair not only in an ethical sense, but also as an unstable feature of capitalism. There would be a tendency by the capitalist class to accumulate more physical capital and use that to augment labor productivity. There would be a tendency to squeeze the wages of labor to increase profits, or there could be a situation where too much of capital could reduce its return, leading to what he referred to as a tendency of the rate of profit to fall. These twin tendencies of falling wages and falling profits could lead to periodic economic crises affecting both the capitalist and the working classes. He predicted that each subsequent crisis would be more intense than the previous one contributing to social and political unrest. He also predicted that, as the working class would be the most oppressed and would have the least to lose, it would emerge out of theses crises as a class that wielded ultimate political power. When this took place, it would define a new system of property rights and production.

An interesting fact of capitalism and its spread was marked by dissimilarities in its impacts in different parts of the world. The effect of industrialization and modernity within Europe was quite different from the impact it had in the Americas, Asia, and Africa. Many of these parts of the world went through prolonged periods of colonial domination by the European countries. By the middle of the 20th century, most of these countries were characterized as having gained freedom from the colonial rulers, but having an economic structure quite different from those in Europe and North America. There was a complex amalgamation of the old and the new with elements of feudalism coexisting with modern capitalism. These economies were also marked by large inequalities of income and wealth. Jet planes and bullock carts, skyscrapers and mud shanties, modern universities and large-scale illiteracy coexisted within the same geography of these prior colonies.

The uneven spread of capitalism across the world led to a large number of scholars within the heterodox tradition to question whether capitalism as a system was really as dynamic as Marx had conceived and whether the inevitability of a working class revolution leading to socialism was realistic. There has been a rich tradition of analyses of these mixed or hybrid economic structures (Furtado 1964; Prebisch 1970). One characteristic of the world economy emphasized within this tradition was the emergence of giant multinational business corporations with activities spread across many parts of the globe. There corporations are often larger in economic size than many small and medium nations. According to many analysts within this tradition, the power of these large corporations is more than that of nation states. These corporations, through persuasive advertisements, influence and control households' preferences and the choices they make. This has led to a culture of consumerism among citizens where an individual's status, self-confidence, satisfaction, and even the sense of being get defined by the ability to consume (Sinha 2004).

Both the conventional wisdom and the heterodox tradition discussed so far does talk about the possibility of a particular teleology of economic development. In the conventional wisdom, a mature market economy with high levels of income is considered to be the endpoint of economic development with pure economic growth and technological change being the metrics of interest. The Marxian tradition also has a teleology where capitalism would be replaced by socialism and the real history of humankind would begin. On the other hand, another distinct school of thought within the heterodox tradition, referred to as post modernism, denies the existence of any teleological grand design (Milberg 1988; Butler 2002). In its view, development and change do not follow any particular pattern. There are certain structures or elements of an economy or societies that get re-ordered and appear to be different though they are essentially the same. It is like a kaleidoscope, where the designs keep changing with the same set of glass pieces. Hence, to them, understanding development is getting acquainted with a set of contextual stories of how change came about. Fortuitous events are more important than human agency in shaping long-term social change.

Implications of Sustainability on Development

From our discussion, it should be apparent that improvements in the quality of life constitute the most important aspect of economic development. The quality of life depends not only on one's consumption of material goods and services, but also on non-material goods and services such as viewing a beautiful rainbow, the ability to share one's sorrow, having access to a support system, or enjoying a walk in the woods. Thus, in addition to adequate income, a stable society and a healthy environment play an important role in determining human wellbeing, and hence development. These ideas underpin the concept of sustainable development.

The notion of modern-day *sustainability* resonates with the classical economists' concerns about the limits to growth and their predictions of a stationary state. The stationary state, exhibiting zero rate of growth, is a sustainable one because the economy reproduces itself over time. Later, developments in the economic theory explored the possibilities of continuous positive rates of growth that could actually increase over time (Romer 1994, Jones and Vollrath 2013). In this framework of analysis, there were no natural limits to growth. Hence, in a trivial sense, the economy is not only sustainable, but could continue to improve over time with positive and even rising rates of growth. A question that inevitably follows is whether the physical growth of material goods (essentially value-added outcomes of finite natural resources), which is of fundamental importance in economic development, can continue indefinitely. While it may be possible for a firm or community or even a nation, it must necessarily be constrained by the fixity of the total amount of resources available on the planet—not only land, as identified by the classicists, but also exhaustible and non-renewable resources like fossil fuels and mineral ores. Essential renewable resources, like trees in the forests, marine fish stock, can become exhausted depending on the mismatch between the rate of utilization and rate of regeneration. It is also well known now that production and consumption of material goods often create damage to the natural environment through pollution and wastes. Hence, the importance of the natural environment and how it is used by the economic processes is essential in understanding to what extent material growth can continue.

Within the heterodox tradition, Marx (1959/1844) and Engels (1908, 1940) had a clear idea that the capitalist mode of production would have a lasting adverse impact on nature, particularly by over use of natural resources. This was despite technological innovations improving the productivity of resources. However, Marx's concerns were more immediate in terms of the potential conflict between the interest of the capitalists and the wellbeing of the workers, which would ultimately lead to a revolution replacing capitalism with a fairer and less destructive system. In the backdrop, Marx's understanding of history clearly appreciated the fundamental importance of the relationship of human beings with nature. To Marx, capitalism was not a sustainable system for more reasons than one.

Questions about the man–nature relationship within this tradition have been recently revived with scholars of radical ecology contributing to a critique on capitalism's impact on the natural environment (Foster 2002; Chester 2013).

The aforementioned discussions on what constitutes economic development and whether the process can be sustained over time leads us to a basic philosophical query, which has important practical implications: What do we (human beings living on the planet earth) owe to ensure the wellbeing of future generations? Depending on the answer to this question, our current actions will be determined in terms of what bequests we leave for people who are not yet born. The answer is not an easy one. Individual opinions would differ, ranging from owing absolutely nothing to the future generations to giving up all current wellbeing to ensure maximum wellbeing in the future and a host of intermediate responses in terms of the sacrifices to be made and costs to be borne by the present generation.

Sustainable development is about ensuring the potential *continuity* of human wellbeing over generations. It should not, however, adversely affect contemporaneous development outcomes. It must necessarily give due importance to correcting material deprivations of the present generation. Sustainable development is all about balancing economic development and human wellbeing within the current generation, as well as across generations to come in the future. It is a complex problem. It will require looking at the wellbeing of humanity as an essential part of the ability of nature to regenerate itself along with all other forms of life.

The economics of sustainable development encompasses many facets of economics, ranging from the political economy to development economics to ethical concerns to designing mechanisms to influence individual behavior. In the chapters that follow, we shed light on each of these aspects, providing simple illustrations and examples from the real world as applicable. To start with, we situate sustainable development at the intersection of economic activity and natural processes, discussing the need to appreciate the interrelationship between the two so as to understand the concept itself. Chapter 3 brings in the notion of the future and determining future outcomes in terms of decisions taken today. Sustainable development is about reducing intergenerational and intra-generational inequality. Some of the complexities of this dynamic decision-making are looked at in Chapter 4, focusing on the importance of homogeneity with respect to access to resources and opportunities. Sustainable development must be a characteristic of nature as a whole, of which human beings are but a small part. The next chapter takes a nuanced view of sustainable development, highlighting two different schools of thought on what actions may constitute sustainable initiatives. Chapter 6 examines some available measures of sustainable development and the impact of human activity on nature. Chapters 7 and 8 look at detailed economics of markets, government policies, and corporate strategies. How markets fail and how policies may be used to internalize the negative externalities caused by economic progress in the material sense is the subject matter of Chapter 7. The role of business corporations in the context of sustainable development is briefly explored next. This includes reacting to stakeholder pressures, regulatory policies, and as a competitive strategy, including self-enlightened behavior. The next chapter is entirely devoted to what arguably constitutes the most perplexing environmental problem facing humankind, namely, climate change. It is an important example of the classical problem of collective action failure. Solutions are known and generally accepted, but getting nations (even communities within them) to take concrete steps becomes an almost intractable problem. Chapter 10 discusses both the importance of collective action at the global level, as well as some of the constraints of the international political economy to arrive at a universally acceptable strategy toward sustainability. Some of the ethical issues that are germane to sustainable development are looked at in Chapter 11. These are usually rights and obligations that human beings have to all other forms of life, including human beings not yet born. These issues are not easy to resolve in a clear unambiguous way. However, it is the living generations' moral agency that will determine one out of the many possible future outcomes. A fundamental question raised by many scholars pertains to whether business as usual under market capitalism can ever lead to a sustainable path of development. The final chapter, Chapter 12, briefly reviews some of the literature on what is termed *radical ecology*, which tries to imagine alternative socioeconomic structures.

CHAPTER 2

Economic Activity and Nature

In order to understand the concept of sustainability, there is a need to enrich our understanding of the intricate relationship between human activity and nature. On the one hand, there is an obvious and important role that nature plays in improving human wellbeing. On the other hand, human activities have the potential to alter nature in the way we live and work. Human beings are an integral part of nature, and hence, the relationship should not be viewed as one between two distinct independent entities. Different branches of knowledge view humans and nature differently. For example, the physical sciences of physics and chemistry focus only on nature, while social sciences, such as political science, study only humans and their interactions. Subjects such as biology, ecology, and economics recognize the interrelationship between nature and humankind, but the extent of focus on each differs. In this chapter, we will first discuss how nature is perceived and treated in mainstream economic analysis. This will then be contrasted with the ecologists' view.

The Economists' Perspective

Put very simply, the economist is accustomed to viewing nature as something to be used for the benefit of humankind. This anthropogenic view looks at the entirety of nature as resources that can be exploited and used. As far as useful resources are concerned, nature is considered to be an inexhaustible gift hamper. Not only that, the wastes we produce through production and consumption activities are dumped in nature as if it were a garbage-bin of infinite capacity. Nature and the natural environment have been considered to be outside the economic system, providing a constant and stable background for economic activity. The availability of natural resources, whether non-renewable like coal or oil, or renewable like forests or fish, is assumed not to pose any constraints to economic growth, and ecosystem services like clean air, abundant water, and assimilation of wastes are supposed to be unlimited. These assumptions were reasonably accurate for the world in the 19th century, given the scale of economic activity and population pressure. However, in the last few decades, the rate of growth of economic activity has brought about a stress on the availability of natural resources and ecosystem services. What appeared unlimited earlier is now being predicted by experts to become binding constraints in the near future.

Formal analysis in economics looks at incremental (marginal) changes, only rendering it ill-equipped to handle large changes in natural resource availability and wastes. When we think about production of goods or services, it is obvious that natural resources are essential inputs in material production. Physical capital stock is built from available natural inputs and labor. Labor, in turn, requires inputs of food (produced from natural resources) to be able to expend energy to work. Despite this essential role of natural products, the economic analysis of production fails to explicitly recognize the changing availability of these resources. Even today, all textbooks of basic economic theory look at the activity of production as being determined by the inputs of physical capital and labor alone. The knowledge of how to combine these resources is available in the form of a technology that transforms capital and labor into physical goods. The standard notation used is $Y = F(K,L)$, where K and L stand for physical capital and labor, respectively, and F embodies the technology transformation function. Y represents the material goods or services produced. Material resources and energy, although essential in production, are found missing in the abstract representation of the production function.

The primary economic problem is to maximize production (or consumption, or exchange) of goods, whether it is for an economy as a whole or even constituent units such as households and business firms. This maximization is subject to the availability of resources with the degree of scarcity reflected in their prices and the state of knowledge embodied in technology. The process of production and consumption is reflected in a familiar schematic diagram referred to as the circular flow of goods and incomes (see Figure 2.1). The constituent units of the economy are taken

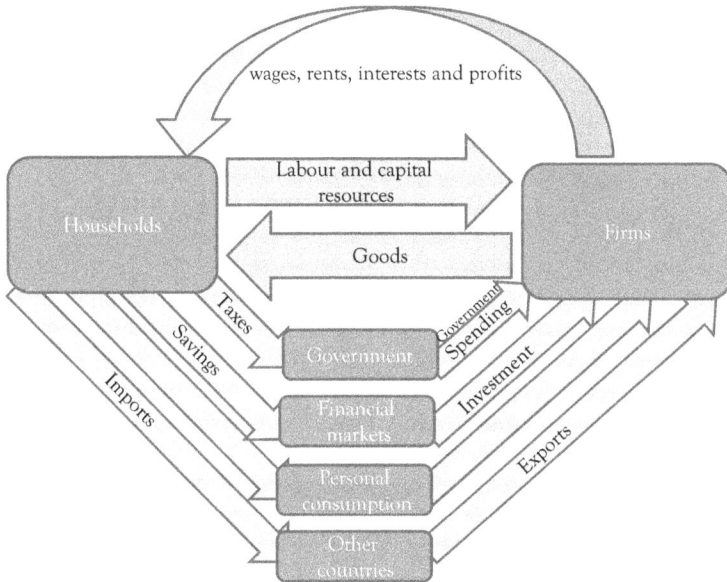

Figure 2.1 The circular flow model of an economy

to be households and firms connected through the social institution of markets. The households own labor and capital resource services, which they offer to the firms. In return, they receive income in the form of wages, interest, profit, and rent from firms. The firms use the labor and capital to make goods and services that are purchased by the household (and other firms) with the income they have earned. The circular flow accommodates other important institutions, like the government and banks, and international trade in the form of exchange with other countries of the world. The circular flow is a basic diagram used in almost all textbooks of economic theory, but as is evident from the diagram, there is no explicit mention of the natural environment or resources used and wastes created in the whole process.

Even if one modified Figure 2.1 to bring in nature as a reservoir of resources and a sink for wastes, the best representation would probably be as has been depicted in Figure 2.2. The diagram shows that the economy depends on nature for both ecosystem services and raw materials. Examples of ecosystem services and amenities would be water supply, climate regulation, soil building, and recreation facilities offered by nature's bounty. Raw materials could be extracted and processed, or harvested,

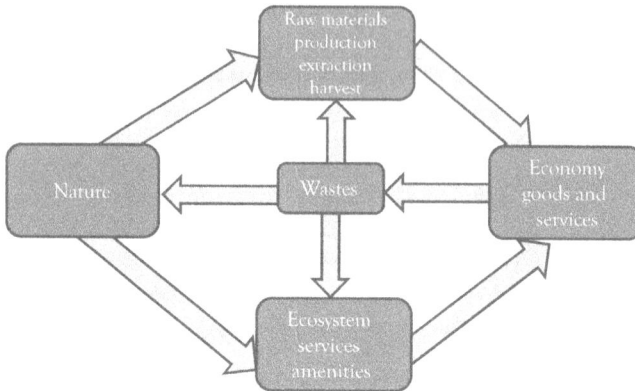

Figure 2.2 Economy and nature: The economists' view

from renewable and non-renewable resources. Firms process the services and raw materials to return wastes to nature. There is no consideration of any limit to the availability of resources and amenities from nature or of nature's ability to process wastes.

The institution of markets plays a critical role in the transactions between firms and households buying and selling resources, as well as goods and services. The act of exchange presupposes private property rights. When a consumer buys a good, the property right over the good is transferred from the producer to the consumer. Markets are a place where buyers and sellers voluntarily meet to transact and the price of the good or service transacted depends both on the strength of the demand and supply. In such a market, if the good (or resource in question) being transacted becomes more scarce for some reason, then its supply will shrink, and the price will rise, given the state of demand. The market treats scarcity as a situation of falling supply, and hence makes the good more expensive through rising prices. In some cases of natural resources, the supply may be so high relative to demand that the market is unable to determine a positive price of the good. Such goods are usually referred to as "free goods", such as oxygen in ambient air, and hence, no markets are observed in such situations. The pricing mechanism for a regular good and a free good has been shown in Figure 2.3.

In situations where supplies cannot be further augmented, society would be looking for substitutes of the good in question that can serve

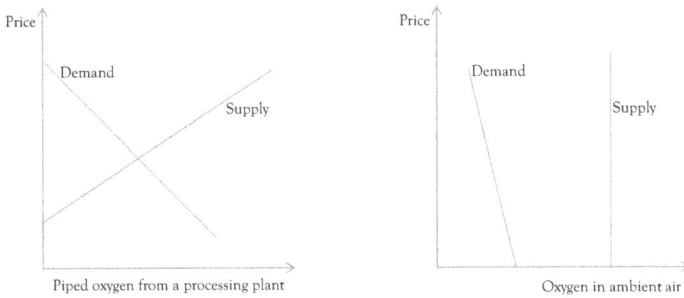

Figure 2.3 *Price discovery: Role of scarcity and property rights*

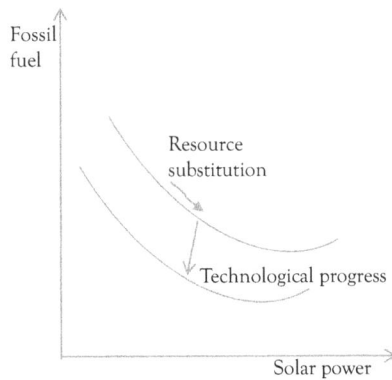

Figure 2.4 *Technological progress and resource substitution as responses to scarcity*

the same purpose. For instance, if fossil fuels become scarcer and cannot be renewed, there would be a sharp increase in their price. In response, society would look for alternative resources such as solar or wind power for meeting their energy needs. Another way society might react to a situation of scarcity is to make the use of the resource more efficient through technological innovations. For instance, automobile engines that use gasoline derived from fossil fuel might be made more efficient, so that they could run the same distance using a lower amount of fuel. The twin responses to scarcity, namely, resource substitution and technical progress, can be easily depicted in a simple diagram (Figure 2.4), found in almost any introductory textbook of economic theory. In Figure 2.4, while both fossil fuel and solar power are required to generate a unit of electricity, there are different combinations of inputs possible. As one moves toward the right of the unit isoquant[1] (a curve depicting different combinations of fossil fuel and solar power that can produce a unit of electricity), fossil fuel is substituted by solar power, which would be the case as prices of fossil fuel rise because of its relative scarcity. Alternately, technological progress may result in a shift to the lower unit isoquant. The lower unit isoquant represents greater efficiency because the unit of electricity can be produced with lower amounts of both kinds of inputs.

Although it would appear from the discussion so far that economists have been oblivious to environmental issues arising from natural resource use or wastes created (pollution) during production or consumption, this is not entirely correct. Pigou (1964) writing in the 1920s analyzed the implications of third-party or bystander effects, or externalities as economists refer to them. For instance, a private producer of chemicals might produce noxious fumes as a by-product in making the chemicals. These fumes are let out into the atmosphere, and neighbors residing close to the factory could suffer medical problems by inhaling the fumes. The cost to society (in this case, the medical costs) are not borne by the producer of the pollution. Hence, market prices do not reflect these additional costs, leading to a reduction in overall welfare. Methods were designed to internalize this cost; the details of which will be discussed later in Chapter 7.

While concern with pollution damage was relatively new in the early–mid 20th century, the implications of resources being scarce and fixed in availability were addressed by the classical writers mainly in the context of land and depletion of resources like coal and fish (Jevons 1906). Later, issues arising out of resource scarcity were formalized into mainstream economics through solving for the optimal rate of use and depletion of an exhaustible resource and determination of optimal harvest rates for renewable resources (Hotelling 1931; Dasgupta and Heal 1979).

Thus, while economists recognized the concerns and limits to growth that the ecological environment could impose, they dealt with these issues by modifying their pre-existing framework of demand and supply

---

[1] A unit isoquant is a set different combination of inputs that will be able to produce one unit of the output. For instance, one could think of all the different combinations of polyester and cotton that would produce one sq. m of textile.

for optimal resource allocation. While this may have led to obtaining solutions in terms of incremental changes, it has not been able to address the larger problems of the aggregate limits imposed by the ecosystem. Without a change in the analytical framework itself, it would be difficult to comprehend and analyze nature–human interrelationships fully. The depletion of resources and the accumulation of wastes need to be treated as an integral part of the production function of an economy (Chambers and Guo 2009; Daly 1996). However, if one looks at the bulk of economic research, one observes that the focus continues to be on tweaking the existing framework. One reason for this could be that the demand–supply framework is quite adequate in addressing immediate short-term resource allocation concerns for the wellbeing of society.

A more appropriate framework would have to begin with the assumption that the planet is finite and growth with the help of physical resources cannot be indefinitely sustained. The second assumption would be that human beings cannot treat the relationship with nature as one of one-way dependence, that is, using nature for society's benefits. In using resources and dumping wastes, nature also gets altered, and these changes have consequences for human wellbeing. Hence, economists need to understand ecology and ecosystems much better for a comprehensive understanding of economic activities and their impact on and interdependence with nature in the long haul.

The Ecologists' Perspective

The link between human beings and nature could be viewed in different ways. One popular view described by Boulding (1966) treats the link like a cowboy would treat his surroundings, with "illimitable plains" used in a "reckless, exploitative, romantic and violent" manner. In contrast, Boulding's own view was to stress on the "closed" economy of planet earth, viewed as a single spaceship with no access to unlimited reserves. Thus, Boulding proposed the counterview that improvements in welfare were related to conservation and more optimal use of limited natural resources and energy. Improvements in welfare were not merely synonymous with greater availability of goods and services.

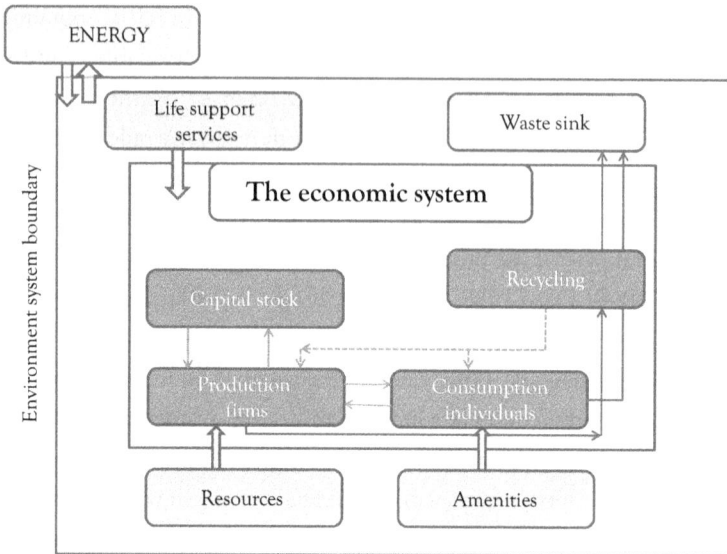

Figure 2.5 The economy in the environment

This basic understanding that resources are finite because the planet earth is a closed system[2], other than inputs of solar radiation, is the basic premise of the ecologists' perspective of the economy. Figure 2.5 attempts to depict this mutually interdependent relationship between nature and the economic system comprising human activities. As can be observed, the economy is embedded within the planetary environment, which is closed, except for the movement of solar energy across its borders. The planetary environment acts as a source of natural resources, as inputs into production, and as a sink for wastes. Two other contributions of the ecosystem, not explicitly recognized by economists, are the life-support services (for example, supply of clean air, fresh water, and moderation of climate) and amenities (services such as fishing, bird watching, observing wildlife, and camping) are essential for human activity to flourish. This is

---

[2] The economy is an example of an open system, which exchanges both matter and energy from its environment. In comparison, the planet earth is a closed system that exchanges only energy from its environment. The universe is an instance of an isolated system that exchanges neither matter nor energy from its environment.

because these services are considered to be free, that is, no market exists for these services as they appear to be unlimited in supply.

In analyzing the closed planetary system, ecologists keep some basic principles in mind (Common and Stagl 2005). The first is that living matter and the physical and chemical environment in which they live exhibit interdependence. The second is that, while continuous transformation of matter and energy takes place, the physical systems of the economy and ecology cannot grow indefinitely. Third, there exists ecological succession, that is, the natural propensity of an ecosystem to become more and more complex over time. This results in the transition of ecosystems from simple and relatively unstable to more stable, diverse, and complex ones. Hence, it is important to preserve biodiversity from the stability point of view. The fourth principle is that, in any ecosystem, nature picks a keystone species, usually the most important one. Finally, despite the notion of a keystone species, many species co-exist. Hence, there has to be sharing, and one species cannot appropriate all resources.

An ecosystem is defined as a community of living organisms known as biota, and their non-living or abiotic environment, and all the interactions between biotic and abiotic components. At the global level, the physical environment consists of the lithosphere (outer shell of the earth), the hydrosphere (water on or near the earth's surface), and atmosphere (gases surrounding the earth's surface). The biosphere comprises all living organisms with their immediate physical environment, described earlier. The biosphere is the biggest (or global) ecosystem. Ecosystems may differ in size, and their specific boundaries may be hard to delineate. For instance, we could talk about ecosystems of a small lake, a big forest, or even a city created by human beings. If ecosystems have a tendency to evolve through succession, an important feature of the systems must be their resilience (up to a point) when they can recover from stress to their original functioning. Too much stress can destroy resilience, and hence, jeopardize the stability of the entire ecosystem.

In the ecosystem, the abiotic components like soil develop as a result of the complex interaction of plant, animal, and microbial communities. They then provide the habitat (space) and immediate source of water and air for the biotic components. The abiotic components also provide six most important elements for life: oxygen, carbon, hydrogen, nitrogen, phosphorus, and sulfur, constituting 95 percent of all living matter. These elements are fixed in supply and have to be recycled because they are critical to the welfare of all ecosystems.

Ecosystems are useful to human society because of the services they provide. These could range from pollination for the bee keeper, soil building and maintenance, and biological control of pests and diseases for the farmer. It could also include recreation, education, and spiritual awareness for the discerning traveler. Other services include climate regulation, water supply regulation, and pollution control. Nature provides these services through recycling and processes known as bio–geo–chemical cycles, such as the nitrogen cycle, carbon cycle, water cycle, and phosphorus cycle, to decompose matter into its constituent abiotic elements.

Ecosystems are characterized by certain properties that contain certain lessons for the economist. Mutual interdependence is an important property of the biosphere (of which human beings are an integral part) where continuous transformations of mass and energy take place governed by a set of natural laws. In these transformations, matter can be recycled indefinitely, but energy cannot. Hence, natural processes are marked by reusing and recycling of all resources, including wastes.

Left on their own, ecosystems exhibit changes in the species compositions that occupy a given area in a period of time. These constant changes are not always predictable or linear in progression. At the pioneer or primary stage, the ecosystem is populated by only a few species, with uncomplicated interrelationships. At this stage, ecosystems are highly vulnerable to environmental stress. These changes eventually lead to a "climax" where diversity, stability, and resilience are observed without a net change in the amount of energy and matter in the system. Changes do occur again, but mature systems usually last long, over a few hundred years. The inter-dependencies could be simple like a food chain or more complex like a food web. The dynamic equilibrium attained exhibits a lack of change in its biotic components. This mature community is called a biome. These changes are not yet fully understood by humans.

As part of nature, human beings also keep altering the ecosystem, both the biotic and abiotic components. This can have varied impacts on the ecology. First, human economic activity can be considered to take place in three stages, from extracting natural resources, to transforming the natural resources to goods, and finally, the returning of wastes to the ecosystem. In these three stages of material transformation, low-entropy[3] matter from the ecosystem is transformed into high-entropy wastes that are returned to nature, compromising the ability of natural resources to be transformed to useful goods and services by humans in the next cycle. As matter is finite and cannot be created, what economists refer to as creation of goods in an economy is actually a transformation of matter. Waste is also part of the matter–energy transformation process and normally poses no problem because it is decomposed back to useful elements and heat energy, which is dissipated through the atmosphere into space, unless prevented from exiting by greenhouse gases such as carbon dioxide. Energy, however, cannot be recycled like matter can.

Second, human beings consciously intervene to change ecosystems. It is in this sense that human beings often play the role of Mother Nature even though the full import of their actions is unknown to them. Economic activities such as agriculture, mining, industrial manufacturing, and the development of urban space all create changes in the natural ecosystems. These changes are manifested in deforestation for agriculture, invading the earth's crust to extract resources for mining, over-use of exhaustible resources and creation of wastes, and the development of a built environment of cities with their buildings, roads, and gardens. These result in changed land use patterns, increasing loss in biodiversity, and in the net, a "simplification" of the complex ecosystems, making them much more vulnerable to natural shocks. Yet, the man-made paddy fields, urban playgrounds, and concrete jungles are as much a part of the evolving ecosystems as the disappearing wetlands or the endangered animal and bird species.

These pervasive human interventions, while having adverse effects on natural ecosystems, have been the outcome of economic development and higher levels of human wellbeing. For instance, intensive agriculture has resulted in use of chemical fertilizers, toxic chemicals in herbicides,

---

[3] Entropy is the measure of the level of disorder in a closed, but changing system. In such a system, energy can be transferred in one direction only, from an ordered state to a disordered state. Higher the entropy, higher the disorder and lower the availability of the system's energy to do useful work.

insecticides and fungicides, and overuse of ground water degrading natural ecosystems. Encroaching on the natural habitat of other species has resulted in an alarming loss of biodiversity. The plantations, orchards, and the practice of monoculture have also done irreparable damage to agricultural ecosystems and soil fertility. In many cases, non-native species have been introduced into ecosystems that have outcompeted and displaced keystone species changing the natural composition of the biota. Industrial production and consumption have depleted exhaustible resources to extents where renewability has been jeopardized. This is referred to as ecological overshoot. Other chemical wastes from non-biodegradable plastics, DDT, dioxins, and nuclear waste have continually increased ecological stress. Taken together, all these have not only lowered resilience, but also threatened the survival of local, regional, and even, global ecosystems. Human interventions in nature have been particularly severe and rapid in the last 200 years with the advent of industrial modern societies. In many ways, human beings' mastery of nature has increased manifold, and we might even claim to have taken over nature. The human economic enterprise prevents natural ecological succession in the sense that human technology and society have been breakers of climaxes.

Ecologists are interested in investigating this tension between the interruptions in natural environmental development caused by human activity and the rapid pace of economic development where human societies enjoy ever-growing levels of consumption of material goods and services, which makes life more comfortable and improves wellbeing. This tension has become aggravated with rapid resource and energy using technological changes as well as a growth in population from 1 billion people 200 years ago to over 7 billion people today. For economists, the tension is at best completely absent or at worst entirely manageable through appropriate technological changes and economic policies.

Bringing Together the Two Perspectives

In order to better understand the complex interrelationship between human beings and nature, we need to combine the two perspectives. The economists' view of nature has to be tempered with the learning from ecology about natural processes and the impact of human activity on them. We have already argued that the human–nature relationship is an interactive one, with complex changes in the composition of ecosystems and the services they provide.

While a one-off snapshot of this relationship might provide some useful insights, the interactive aspects can only be appreciated if we look at the change in trends. Even if we consider human activities as a conscious means to improve the nature–human relationship by making it more stable and harmonious, we need to understand how decisions taken today might influence future outcomes. In this sense, economists are competent in analyzing how optimal decisions can be taken in a dynamic framework. In the chapter that follows, we take a brief look at dynamic decision-making and some of its complications and challenges.

CHAPTER 3

Viewing the Future

There is a very obvious reason why even if we do not care about the future at all, our decision to use our capital stock to earn income and consume has an irreversible bearing on outcomes available for future generations. Consider, for instance, a situation where our consumption is exactly the same as our income. Therefore, we do not save at all, not even keeping allowance for replenishing the physical depreciation of the capital stock. As a result, not only would the stock not be augmented, it would decline over time, reducing income, and hence consumption opportunities in the future. Another possibility is that we consume (either through greed or through compulsions of survival) more than the current income, that is, savings are negative (dissaving). In this case too, the capital stock would decline over time (even faster than the previous case), reducing opportunities for the future. We can think of a mid-way situation where we consume our income, but only after setting aside our requirements for the depreciation of capital stock in producing current income. Such a situation would lead to a constant level of capital stock, and hence imply non-diminishing opportunities for future generations. If, however, we have a positive net savings (that is we consume less than our income), then the capital stock of the future would be higher than before, and income opportunities would potentially be larger.

These choices are an outcome of individual decisions taken by households and firms. They are neither taken keeping in view the needs of the current generation as a whole nor by looking at the bequest of possibilities for the future. In these myriad microeconomic decisions, there is no guarantee of any of the aforementioned outcomes being ensured. However, economists observe that, most individual decision-makers do care about the future in a narrow, and perhaps, myopic sense. We can save, keeping in mind the interests of our own children and their immediate future. Or, a firm might plough back profits and grow its business to ensure a better deal for its owners. Hence, most societies are observed to end-up with some positive savings, which explains how they have been surviving across generations.

It is evident from this discussion that a growing (or at least a non-diminishing) capital stock is essential for the survival of future generations. This stock has to be ensured by the current generation as a whole. It is a social problem and cannot be left to individuals, even though most would have a natural propensity to save. For instance, one individual may be affluent, but decide to consume all his or her capital stock, while another individual might be so poor that he or she is compelled to consume his or her capital stock just for survival. Finally, there could be some people in society who do not have access to any source of income. Armed with this knowledge, an immediate question that arises is how much a society needs to save to be able to compensate for the people who do not or are unable to save.

The solution to the social problem of saving is complicated for a number of reasons. First, a social decision to save might involve a degree of coercion or force exerted by the state in the form of higher taxes or lower public spending. This may not be agreeable to all concerned, and there could be resistance to such policies, as some individuals might perceive this as unfair in saving more for the benefit of other people. Second, there could be an argument that technological change that has been so significant in the past 200 years or so is likely to continue into the future. This itself would augment the efficiency of the stock of capital and might not require a great deal of extra saving. Third, there is likely to be a continuation of population growth, which would, in any case, erode the worth of the non-diminishing capital stock because the income generated from it would have to be divided across a greater number of individuals, resulting in a lower per capita value. Fourth, there could be a great deal of uncertainty about the future regarding new knowledge, social institutions, life-styles, and consumer preferences that could lead to a completely different utilization of the capital stock, which cannot be anticipated at the time of taking the decision to save. Fifth, there could be tension between the essential consumption for the current generation and the need to ensure a non-diminishing stock of capital for the future. This tension will be particularly evident in poor societies with low incomes or societies with a high degree of inequality in incomes and wealth. Finally, a deep philosophical question might crop up as to why and to what extent the value of the lives of people who will be born at a later date should affect current decisions. This leads us to problems of whether to discount the future as being less important than the present and whether the present generation has any moral obligation to all future generations of people.

The Social Problem of Saving

We have argued that savings depend on the private decisions of all the households and firms of an economy. These need not add up to any particular level of aggregate savings. Similarly, the government can also save by not spending all the revenue earned from its taxes, but this decision also depends on the compulsions faced by a government by its social obligation to spend and its economic and political limit to levying taxes. Table 3.1 shows wide differences in actual savings observed in different countries in 2014. Hence, if the government decides to have a particular quantum of savings to be used in creating new capital assets for the future, it will have to either increase taxes or reduce public expenditure or both. Neither of these options is usually palatable to society at large. Taxes are often viewed as an act of coercion over which the government has a monopoly right. There are ethical issues pertaining to taxation, especially

Table 3.1 National savings as a per cent of GDP for 2014

Country	Savings as a per cent of GDP
China	49.3
Republic of Korea	34.9
India	31.3
Japan	22.4
France	20
United States	18.4
United Kingdom	12
Kenya	9.6

Source: http://data.worldbank.org/indicator/NY.GNS.ICTR.ZS

if the level of taxation goes beyond the resources required for the provision of basic public services like provision of national defense, ensuring law and order, and protection of property rights. Taxes that benefit citizens in the distant future are quite likely to be disputed and regarded as unfair. Reduction of public expenditure could be considered unethical in situations where these expenditures are used to provide economic entitlements to poor people through services like health, education, and minimal employment opportunities or some form of social security. So, we see that there is a tension between current benefits available to the economy and benefits that will be available at a future date. From a nation, or an entire generation's point of view, both are important, but there could be a thorny debate regarding their relative importance.

One popular argument against the making of current sacrifices for future benefits accruing to another generation is the versatility of human intelligence and enterprise coupled with the pace of technological innovations. Technological changes have made life simpler and resolved many problems of daily living through new products or new processes for using resources more efficiently. Hence, if one factors the possibilities of technological change over time, then the sacrifices required for future benefit may turn out to be less. However, one problem with this argument is, despite every reason to have faith in technological progress, it is very difficult to predict the actual pace and direction of technological change. It may be wise to not depend on technology alone to ensure that resources are conserved, wastes minimized, and there are adequate earnings to sustain people living in the current generation and in all generations to come.

If one factors some estimate of the rate of population growth over time, then the future resources required by a larger community would mean ipso facto a higher sacrifice by the current generation. More capital would be required to produce more income, so that the average or per capita availability of income does not diminish as population grows. Hence, there would be an inhibition to save by individuals not only because the future beneficiaries are unknown, but each individual would have to save for more than one person.

When thinking about distant future requirements, it is often difficult to even imagine the state of affairs that might prevail. This difficulty to even visualize things is often referred to as deep uncertainty. The changes resulting from economic growth, technological progress, and population growth might combine in numerous different ways, leading to completely different outcomes. Some argue that a long span of time might even witness catastrophic events like the earth being hit by asteroids or a global nuclear holocaust. This uncertainty leads people to be wary about making current sacrifices and discounts the costs future generations may have to incur to lead their lives with reasonable material comfort. Those who believe in destiny or in religion might wish to leave the distant future to forces beyond their control, and hence deny the role of human agency in determining the future.

The decision on how much to sacrifice for the future benefits of generations of people will always be constrained by how that decision affects the wellbeing of current generations. It is evident that the sacrifice is made by the current generation as a whole. However, the distribution of the costs within the generation ought to be equitably distributed. It should not worsen existing inequalities and exacerbate material deprivation of people living in poverty. Consider, for instance, a society where the current generation is marked by a low degree of inequality and a very low average income. The economy also has a poor stock of capital. Here, saving for future benefits in terms of more capital formation in the present and more income in the future might require a rate of savings that will not only reduce the average consumption, but also the consumption of the poorest people in that society. The needed redistribution of resources from the present to the future poses a problem if the savings required necessarily reduces the income of the poor people in the current generation.

The social problem of saving, as discussed in the previous paragraphs, can be abstracted into a single larger question related to the importance the current generation assigns to the wellbeing of future generations vis-a-vis their own. Economists (Sen 1984, pp. 113–146) have pointed out that, while savings decisions are at the individuals' level, they may not be entirely against sharing additional costs for a social purpose; say through higher taxes, if the individual is assured that all others in society would do the same. A simple example will suffice to illustrate this assertion. Consider two alternative states of affairs A and B where A has unrestricted pollution in the air and B has almost zero pollution. It is very likely that a set of individuals (households and firms), when asked about their preference, would all prefer B. If individual costs are incurred to reduce the pollution (which the individual can control, say in their own household or firm), it is unlikely that anyone would do so and the social outcome would be A. This is referred to as the isolation paradox, and a transition to B would require costs to be incurred for enforcement of pollution reduction by individuals. However, if an individual is assured that all others are incurring the cost to curb pollution, then he or she will prefer to incur costs to reduce his or her contribution to pollution as well. Hence, the social outcome would be B, which is more desirable, and no enforcement costs would have to be incurred by society. This possibility (referred to as the assurance game) can come about if there is a strict sense of responsibility that citizens have regarding the need to attain B as a social outcome. In this case, it would happen if individuals assign a greater weight to clean air, which would also be bequeathed to future generations.

Economists have tried to quantify the social problem of assigning relative importance to the future generations and their wellbeing through a social discount rate. It is to this discussion that we now turn.

The Ethics of Discounting

Consider a situation where one invests 100 dollars in the bank, where the interest rate of the deposit is 5 percent per annum. At the end of the first year, it would grow to 105 dollars and would compound to 110.25 dollars at the end of the second year. Now, consider a situation where an individual promises to pay us the exact amount of 100 dollars, one year from the present. What would be the maximum amount that individual should set aside to be able to fulfill his or her commitment to us in a year's time? As he or she could earn interest on the amount (at the prevailing rate of 5 percent) if he or she put the money in a bank, he or she could use this as a benchmark for how much money to set aside. This would amount to 95.24 dollars, which, as one would expect, is lower than 100 dollars. 95.24 dollars is the present value of the gift of 100 dollars payable in the future. In this situation, the discounting for the future is done with the help of the interest rate, which may be obtained from the market.

An individual taking this decision would find an easy reference in the observed interest rates in the market place. A much debated question in economics revolves around whether the market interest would be the pertinent number to use for discounting future values when the government measures the valuations society places on consumption that is sacrificed in the present. It is supposed to differ from market-based returns because it has to account for future generations *as a whole* (as opposed to a relatively myopic individual) and involves a kind of paternalism where a senior generation, gifting a junior generation (born later in time) views them as being as important as themselves. This paternalism would then suggest that a discount rate of zero may be the most appropriate approach for taking decisions.

Suppose the social planner chooses a discount rate that is lower than the market interest rate (which would have been chosen by an individual). One has to understand the implications of this choice. For example, if the market interest rate is 10 percent, it implies that the private sector earns 10 percent from marginal investments. The social planner could decide to use a 7 percent discount rate for, let us say, public environmental programs. In that case, such projects would be implemented when they earn more than 7 percent. But, society would lose a return of 10 percent, as resources for investment in the public environment program would come at the cost of lower investments in the private sector. Moreover, consider a situation where the social planner is aware that an asteroid is on course to crash into an emerging market economy, causing damages of over two trillion dollars, 200 years from the present. Using this 7 percent discount rate, the value of preventing such colossal destruction is no more than three million dollars in the present. Such a valuation would be hard to defend. By contrast, a discount rate of 0 percent would indicate that the value of preventing such colossal destruction is two trillion dollars in the present. Alternately, if the social planner decided to use a higher discount rate above 10 percent for environmental projects, say 13 percent, then only those projects would be implemented whose returns exceed 13 percent. The outcome would be that projects with returns between 10 and 13 percent would be rejected, even though they could yield positive net returns. Obviously, the value of preventing destruction because of the asteroid would be much higher than two trillion dollars in the present.

We would argue that the government (represented by the social planner) is distinctly different from a private individual or a business firm. A government's objective is to look at the society as a whole with the wellbeing of current and future generations in mind. Indeed, a nation is considered to live forever. Hence, there has been an argument about the *super responsibility* of government, which has an obligation to the future, which is over and above the sum totals of the private decisions of citizens and firms. The extent of allocation for the future by the government must necessarily exceed the cumulative outcome of all private concerns for the future. Projects for the future can be viewed as gifts made by the current generation by paying taxes to the government. If the government believes that the future generations are important, then it should choose a discount rate that is lower than the market rate (ideally it should be zero). If the government, on the other hand, considers that the importance of future generations diminish, especially when we consider the very distant future, it might opt for a positive, but very low discount rate. This is not because of an intrinsic belief that future generations are less important, but because of deep uncertainties that have to be considered when taking decisions over a very long time horizon.

This discount rate is referred to as the social rate of time preference (r) that reflects society's collective preference for tradeoffs between present and future generations' benefits. There are two ways of looking at r: the first is a utility interpretation, which implies one additional benefit of r today would exactly compensate $(1 + r)$ units of benefit in the future for society as a whole. Alternately, a cost interpretation of r would imply that an additional benefit of r today would be obtained by a reduction of one unit of benefit in the future.

So far, we have been speaking about social wellbeing and social benefits and how to ensure that future social benefit is not compromised. It is necessary to define and understand better what exactly one means by social wellbeing and try and formulate methods by which it can be measured. For this, we need to understand the concepts of social choice and benefits so to arrive at an aggregate function representing social wellbeing that we can maximize.

Social Benefits and Social Choice

Social decisions reflecting a social choice were first systematically studied by French mathematicians of the late 18th century, particularly, Borda (1781) and Marquis de Condorcet (1785).[1] They wanted to identify voting arrangements that would avoid instability and arbitrariness in social choice. This was to formulate voting mechanisms so that democratic decisions of a group addressed the preferences and interests of all its members. However, their results were not satisfactory, and they even found that the well-known majority rule can be quire inconsistent.

Many years later, drawing on Bentham's (1907) work on utility as a subjective state of wellbeing, economists like Edgeworth (1881), Marshall (1920), and Pigou (1964) developed the notion of social welfare by aggregating utilities of individuals to arrive at the total utility of a community or society. The utility of an individual would have to be measurable and be in the same unit for all. The distribution of utility across individuals was irrelevant, and the total utility was all that mattered. Hence, this branch of social choice was deeply concerned with comparing utility gains and losses across individuals. This approach was focused on judging a social outcome exclusively on the basis of changes in total utility. If a change resulted in the loss of utility for a few people, but a net greater gain for others, the total utility would be greater than before and would be a preferred social outcome. It is possible that a change could result in a loss of utility for a large number of people, but a substantial net gain for the remaining few. If, in the net, the total utility increased, this change would also be a socially preferred outcome. It is consequentialist in approach where the outcome in terms of total utility is the only measure that ultimately matters.

Utilitarian welfare was severely criticized for its exclusive focus on total utility and its complete disregard of distributional matters. Economists like Lionel Robbins (1935) extended the critique by pointing out that interpersonal comparisons of utility had no scientific basis because utility was a very subjective concept and personal in nature.

---

[1] This section has drawn heavily from Sen's Nobel lecture.

Every mind is inscrutable to every other mind and no common denominator of feelings is possible

—(Robbins 1935, p. 636)

The non-acceptance of interpersonal comparisons led to the rise of new welfare economics that used only one criterion for social improvement posited by Pareto (1971). Pareto efficiency implies a state of affairs, deviations from which would lead to at least one person becoming worse off, measured in terms of his or her own utility. The deviations would not rule out the possibility of a number of people becoming better off in terms of their own utilities; however, such a situation would not be deemed a social improvement simply because gains and losses could not be netted out. This criteria still remains an important aspect of economists' judgment about the social state of affairs.

To bring greater reach in judging social states of affairs by looking at the preferences of individuals, rather than a utility function, Arrow (1950) pioneered the concept of a social welfare function. This mathematical function was supposed to satisfy some desirable features that would take into consideration the individual preference ordering[2] of all the members of society. These included the notion of Pareto efficiency and a requirement that no individual could act as a dictator. It also required that every individual would have a complete preference ordering across all possible states of affairs, and the social choice over any set of alternatives would depend on the preferences for those alternatives only. Arrow showed that no social welfare function could be constructed to exhibit all these features simultaneously. Later developments in social choice (Sen 2017; Suzumura 1983; Basu, Pattanaik and Suzumara (eds) 1995) have argued that imperfect knowledge, partial ordering, and some limited interpersonal comparisons of utility should not deter society from coming up with a social choice that could lead to actual practical action

---

[2] An individual (typically a consumer) has preferences across alternative goods (or state of affairs) available to him or her. For instance, he or she may prefer tea over coffee and coffee over hot chocolate. Similarly, he or she may prefer winter over a hot summer, or sea beaches over mountain resorts. These preferences are typically over a large variety of possibilities from which he or she could choose. The ranked preferences are called preference orderings.

to achieve an objective. It has been posited that, in important cases where most people consider it urgent that society do something to remedy the situation, consistent results may ensue even in the face of imperfections in the desirable features of a welfare function. It is important to note that the informational content underlying social decisions has to be broadened beyond focusing on individual advantage measured by the metric of utility. This could also help incorporate the use of more objective data than the mental reactions of individuals to a particular outcome.

The Dynamics of Decision-Making

In the earlier sections, we have discussed the importance of saving, the requirements of a social discount rate, and the difficulties of constructing a social welfare function. If society wants to maximize intergenerational welfare over an indefinite future, then it requires some social welfare function to maximize and some discount rate through which the future streams of consumption are valued. Neither the social welfare function nor the social discount rate will be free from subjective judgments and ethical considerations in determining the form of the function and the absolute value of the rate. In solving this dynamic maximization problem, there are bound to be other complications too.

We have already seen that the social rate of time preference would imply that the decision to consume now would be deemed more important than the decision to consume in the future. If investment possibilities exist, then there will be rewards for savings (usually measured by the prevailing market rate of interest) at the cost of reducing current consumption. The rewards for saving will lead to the possibility of consuming more in the future. This, in turn, would imply that society would try to consume a little less now to consume more in the future.

Finally, the nature of the social welfare function with some reasonable properties such as diminishing marginal gains[3] would result in a smooth

---

[3] Diminishing marginal gains follows from the famous economic law of diminishing returns. It means that gains (profits or utility or satisfaction) usually increase with more production or consumption, but at a diminishing rate. In other words, the incremental changes are positive, but declining in magnitude.

distribution of income over time. If marginal gains are diminishing, then a tiny amount of income withdrawn from the future and re-allocated to the present would imply that the loss (of future consumption) would be less than the gain (in current consumption). This is referred to in the economic theory as the *aversion* to inequality.

The dynamic decision problem exerts pulls in three different directions. The social rate of time preference or impatience increases current consumption over future consumption. The possibility of productive investment reduces current consumption in favor of future consumption, and the aversion to inequality has a tendency to equalize current and future consumptions. The solution to the maximization problem would depend on the *combination* of values chosen for the three variables.

How do we arrive at a social welfare function and a social rate of time preference that is representative of society as a whole? Society is essentially an aggregate of a large set of individuals, each of whom has a particular ethical ranking of states of current and future affairs. It would be an easy decision if the social planner knew that a majority of the society had a strong ethical preference for guaranteeing a level of wellbeing for future generations, at least as high as the current generation's. This pattern of preferences is very unlikely to occur in complex heterogeneous societies. The planner's decision, therefore, is unlikely to be based on a consensus. It would necessarily be subjective and could appear to be arbitrary and autocratic.

CHAPTER 4

Inequality and Policy Choices for Sustainable Development

We have argued that sustainable development is essentially about reducing inequalities over time and across generations without affecting the wellbeing of the current generation in any adverse way. The most commonly used definition of sustainable development is due to Brundtland (World Commission on Environment and Development 1987), which states that it is about meeting the needs of the future generations without reducing the ability of the current generation to meet its own needs. Translating this definition into a practically usable proposition is difficult for a number of reasons. For instance, the perception of the needs of a society varies from individual to individual. It also changes over time. We might have many measures of wellbeing. Hence, not only are individuals different from each other, there is a plurality of measures of wellbeing too. In this chapter, we will explore some of these dimensions and see how we can arrive at a more workable understanding of sustainability. In this respect, inequality and its reduction play a critical role.

There could be deep philosophical debates about inequality and its many forms. Social and political philosophers have, however, always emphasized some form of equality across individuals and between societies. Sen (1973) has argued quite persuasively that emphasizing equality in any one aspect among individuals or across societies might open up undesirable inequalities in other spheres. For instance, if we argue that we would like a significantly reduced level of inequality in income and wealth in a society, it might open up greater inequalities in terms of opportunities to earn income and create wealth. Inequality has direct impact on natural resource use and the emission of wastes and pollution. If the current generation consumes more of exhaustible resources and wastes more, then there will be less of resources left to use in the future, worsening intergenerational inequality. If the current generation is characterized by a high degree of inequality in income and wealth, there will be adverse effects on the natural environment even if we ignore what is likely to happen in the future. For instance, the very rich with greater access to natural wealth can consume and waste much more than they need to. It could be in terms of food, fossil fuels, or water. On the other hand, the very poor in their compulsions to survive would have a tendency to overuse whatever little access to natural resources they might have. They could overwork the soil and they could overdraw water for growing crops and they could destroy forests and natural habitats of other species for short-term benefits. In both the cases, the degradation of the natural environment would be much more than a society where the rich could be a little worse off and the poor a little better off, in other words, moving toward more equality. An unequal society in a developing economy is characterized by an implicit subsidy that the poor provide for the rich. An instance of this would be the fact that most of the poor are without access to modern forms of energy such as electricity and cooking gas. As a result, the wastage of energy by the rich who are in the minority is not reflected in per capita energy consumption numbers, which in fact may be quite modest.

Intra- and Intergenerational Inequality

The impact of inequality on wellbeing goes beyond the environmental dimensions of wellbeing. There is a large literature on growing inequality in the contemporary world, both within countries and across countries (Piketty, Thomas, and Goldhammer 2014, 2015; Deaton 2013). High levels of inequality are not only risky for political and social stability, but also damaging for important quality of life indicators such as health, longevity, infant mortality, and mental illnesses. It has also been observed that a lack of social cohesion and the incidence of crime and violence, including violence toward women, are much higher in economically unequal societies. As social mobility is restricted, equality of opportunities is difficult to achieve. There is also evidence that unequal economies (both rich and poor) experience shorter spells of growth and expansion than more equal societies, making them more vulnerable to economic shocks. Inequality makes status competition more intense, which, in turn, leads to a greater social value attached to consumerism. This consumerism is often driven by rising personal debts. The value of community life and collective action are reduced. Arriving at a political consensus and implementing a national or global strategy becomes difficult. Societies with greater equality in income and wealth usually have a better quality of life in terms of health, longevity, and mortality, and people are more willing to act together for the common good.

Apart from these aspects of wellbeing that improve with equality, conditions of lower inequality are more conducive to sustainable development. It may be easier for a more equal society to arrive at a social consensus on any issue, including what might be needed to be done for the wellbeing of future unborn generations. If some resources are to be set aside as savings for the future of all generations, the costs could be borne more equitably where everybody in the current generation might make a similar sacrifice. In an unequal society, asking the poor to pay is unfair. On the other hand, asking the rich to pay might also be unfair to the poor because the living poor would be competing with a faceless future generation for scarce resources. It should be kept in mind that the aforementioned argument in favor of equality is valid only if the current generation, based on its levels of awareness, decides on some course of action for the future generations. An otherwise equal society may reach a consensus to consume and destroy all exhaustible resources. There is nothing the future generation can do to prevent this. Hence, intragenerational equality improves the lives of living people and has the potential to improve the lives of future generations, but does not necessarily translate into intergenerational equality.

Intergenerational equality, in the context of sustainability, implies that future generations' wellbeing should not be worse off than the wellbeing of the current generation. This does not require strict equality across generations. Just as the current generation is, in many ways, materially better off than previous generations, future generations are not restricted from being better off than the current generation. There is no reason to believe that the human ability to be imaginative and innovative would not continue to result in improvements of wellbeing in the future, through better technology or better social institutions. There are some key differences between the philosophical bases for reducing intragenerational inequality and the prevention of deterioration of intergenerational wellbeing. Broadly speaking, they can be divided into two strands of arguments. The former relates to ethical questions of distributive justice. There is also reasonable agreement among philosophers and social scientists' regarding what is to be redistributed and given to the poor. These include income, productive capital, capabilities, knowledge, skills, and rights and liberties. There could be debates about the extent of and the procedure for attaining distributive justice, however. Intergenerational justice is philosophically more problematic to handle. A typical question that is difficult to answer would be whether unborn people have rights and entitlements. Another question would be that what we consider valuable in the present generation (a certain set of assets or amenities) may not be considered valuable in the future. Indeed, the morality of a future society may be entirely different from that prevalent in the present. Hence, the question about what exactly is to be transferred to the future may be difficult to answer.

> *The catch is that today's poor want consumption not investment. So the conflict is pretty deep and there in unlikely to be any easy way to resolve it…..research is a good thing. Knowledge on the whole is an environmentally neutral asset that can contribute to the future…. Investment in the broader sense and investment in knowledge, especially technological and scientific knowledge, is as environmentally clean an asset as we know. And the last thing I want to say is, don't forget that sustainability is a vague concept. It is intrinsically inexact. It is not something that can be measured out in coffee spoons. It is not something that you could be numerically accurate about. It is, at best, a general guide to policies that have to do with investment, conservation and resource use. And we shouldn't pretend that it is anything other than that.*

—(Solow 1991, p. 138)

In the section that follows, we discuss some of the contentious ethical issues related to intergenerational justice.

The Ethics of Intergenerational Equity

Modern economic growth has had deleterious effects on the natural environment that are likely to be persistent, or have materialized after decades or centuries. Typical examples would be that of radioactive wastes or greenhouse gas emissions. These problems have triggered greater interest about intergenerational justice among economists. This discussion presupposes a number of things. First of all, it assumes that human beings will live forever. Second, it assumes that some form of technological improvement and progress will continue to characterize change. Finally, it presupposes that we do have some obligation to minimize harm caused to people yet unborn. Each of these suppositions can be questioned because of the fundamental asymmetry in the relationship between a living generation and an unborn generation. Many philosophers argue that rights and entitlements can characterize a living being. If the concept of duty is considered to emerge from interaction among human beings and not in any abstract hypothetical context, then people of the future have no rights or claims on the people of the present. There is another difficulty that arises when we consider a hypothetical human-being inhabiting the planet at a future date. Philosophers have pointed out that, if that a hypothetical individual faces difficulties in leading a reasonably trouble-free life (because of environmental pollution, for example), she cannot logically blame it on the current generation. The reason is simple. If the current generation had taken a different decision regarding environmental pollution, the world would have been different, with different resources, and a different population. There is no guarantee that, in that world, the hypothetical individual would have been born at all. Therefore, two different consumption (or saving) decisions taken by the current generation are not comparable because their outcomes would be experienced by two different population sets in the future.

An alternative approach would be to seek some moral justification for an action that values the wellbeing of future generations. One way of doing this would be to extend the Rawls (1971) concept of a social contract drawn up from an *original position* on the basis of the *veil of ignorance*.[1] One might, in this context, think of all humanity, born and unborn, getting into a social contract behind a *veil of ignorance* where it is known with certainty that some individuals will be better off than others and inequality could be significant. However, there is complete uncertainty regarding the fate of each individual in terms of actually being better off or worse off. Hence, the Rawlsian argument for providing maximum resources or wellbeing for the minimally positioned individual could be the basis of the social contract drawn up. There would be a universal consensus on this because each individual has an equally probable chance of being that minimally positioned individual, and hence the beneficiary of such a scheme. This argument provides an ethical justification for caring about the future. One might look at different individuals with different levels of wellbeing, where the wellbeing of the worst off individual would have to attain a certain minimum level. In a similar vein, philosophers like Pletcher (1981), Meyer (2003), and Passmore (1980) have argued that concern for the future, such as some general obligations to minimize harm, can be considered as justifying the provision of a minimum amount of care for future generations. The ethical basis for reducing intragenerational inequalities is very similar.

From Individual to Social Wellbeing

The measurement of intergenerational wellbeing requires some simplifying assumptions to extract certain operational directives. We will assume that each individual in a generation has a wellbeing function where the determining variable is the state of affairs faced by the individual. Each individual's wellbeing can be represented by a numerical index. These

---

[1] The *original position* refers to a philosophical prior to the formation of a society. Individuals know the social outcomes, but are uncertain about their own exact position in the order of things. Hence, in the *original position,* each individual is constrained by the *veil of ignorance* in not knowing the exact economic condition that would be realized for him or her.

indices can be aggregated to compute the numerical value of the generation's social wellbeing.

Let us assume that each individual in a society has a wellbeing function denoted by W, and the level of W is a function of the state of affairs faced by the individual. Consider a set X of states of affairs with elements like A, B, C …. There are N individuals in the society, each indexed by i, that is, the wellbeing of the ith individual would be W_i. When the social state is C, social wellbeing is assumed to be the sum total of all the individuals wellbeing, denoted by

$$U(C) = W_1(C) + W_2(C) + \ldots\ldots + W_N(C).$$

If we now consider different generations for all time (from now to infinity) and we assume that the current generation (t) values the wellbeing of all future generations (t + 1, t + 2,….), then we can define the intergenerational wellbeing function in the following way.

$$V_t = U(C_t) + U(C_{t+1}) + \ldots\ldots U(C_\infty), \text{ or } V_t = \Sigma_t^\infty U(C_t) \text{ for t } \geq 0,$$
where t = 0 represents the current generation.

As is evident, for a generation in time period t, the state of affairs is assumed to be C, which includes the consumption of food, clothing, and shelter and access to legal aid, health care, education opportunities, leisure activities, political and civil liberties, and direct amenities from the environment. It has also been generally assumed that the current generation maximizes intergenerational wellbeing, V_t.[2] This formulation has been used by several economists to arrive at a dynamic solution, which could determine all future states of affairs. A solution exists to this mathematical formulation, which is a set of states of affairs, $\{C_0^*, C_1^*, C_2^*, \ldots\ldots C_\infty^*\}$.

This was first used by Frank Ramsey in 1928 in a paper where he sought the answer to the question of the level of a nation's savings. Unlike an individual, a nation is supposed to live forever and to achieve that, something from current income would have to be left for the future.

---

[2] The problem reduces to maximizing $V_t = \Sigma_t^\infty U(C_T)$ for t ≥ 0.

Hence, his famous question, "How much should a Nation save?" Ramsey was not concerned with sustainability explicitly. Yet, he was actually solving for a stream of optimal consumption that could be sustained by society over a long period of time. Ramsey made an important assumption that future human beings were as important as us, the current generation, and hence, their wellbeing should not be discounted just due to the accident of having a later date of birth.

Ramsey made another assumption that wellbeing increased with increases in C, but at a diminishing rate. This assumption is a standard one in economics, analogous to the concept of diminishing marginal utility. His formulation could readily accommodate two aspects of a real society, namely, uncertainty about the future and demographic growth. In the former case, wellbeing would have to be reinterpreted as expected wellbeing with some prior probabilities assigned to different states of affairs. In the latter case, with population growth, C, the state of affairs would have to be defined in per capita terms and the function W suitably reinterpreted. The alternative formulations discussed would all yield a solution in terms of a set of states of affairs with similar properties. An important property of the Ramsey result was that if each generation maximized intergenerational wellbeing, then the current generation's choice of the set of Cs would exactly match the choice of the future generations. This is a remarkable result, with the property referred to as exhibiting ethical congruency, where the current generation's treatment of future generations is exactly the same as the future generation's treatment of their future generations. Ramsey showed that when the t = 1 generation came, they would choose C^*_1 and t = 2 would choose C^*_2 and so on. Each generation would choose its optimum knowing that succeeding generations would choose according with what it had planned for them.

The Sustainability Condition

We can think of the starting condition of the Ramsey formulation as a generation that has inherited a stock of productive resources from the past, including natural resources, population, produced capital, institutional infrastructure, knowledge, and technology. This stock provides a flow of income from which the generation chooses C^*_0 for consumption and saves the rest for the next generation. It may be noted that C_0^* could be the entire stock of net national product.[3] If the initial net national product is entirely consumed, it is still a sustainable outcome where the maximum current level of consumption can be reproduced forever. The net national product is the flow of income that can be generated or saved from the stock of assets that the society possesses. It is clear that C_0^* must be sufficient to meet the survival needs of the current generation.

The Ramsey result may lead to some obvious questions about practical issues such as what qualifies as the survival needs of the current generation and concern for generations that will come after an infinitely long period of time. The issue of discounting has also been raised regarding the need to treat the very distant future as something clearly less important than our own needs in the here and now. There could be several responses to these concerns; for instance, if we know that the world will not be there forever, considering the infinite future does not make tangible sense, it would still remain a matter of great uncertainty as to when the end would come. Without precise knowledge of that date, we cannot decide on the terminal period where our allocation exercise would end. As far as discounting is concerned, if we do agree that the future is less important, then reworking the Ramsey formulation with a positive rate of discount could lead to an outcome where the consumption or wellbeing of a future generation could come down to zero. This result would hold if society had some exhaustible resources. This possibility as an outcome appears to be ethically unacceptable. However, if one concedes to a position that one might choose a very low rate of discount, then the future where consumption is driven down to zero could arrive at a very distant date. For instance, we could pick a discount rate low enough so that the disappearance of consumption occurs, say, a billion years from now. Most people would agree that a billion years is a sufficiently long time within which other uncertain events could be realized such as the earth being destroyed by an asteroid.

These issues would not have been of great concern had not the Ramsey result implied two problems. The first relates to the answer to the

---

[3] Net national product is the total output of the economy after accounting for depreciation of the entire stock of productive assets.

question he raised in his seminal paper, how much should a nation save. On the basis of plausible parameter values for the global economy, quick calculations reveal that the optimal rate of savings has to be somewhere near 60 percent of the global GDP (Dasgupta 2001, p. 93). No country saves 60 percent and most countries savings rates are significantly lower than even 40 percent (see table in Chapter 3). This restricts the applicability of the Ramsey model to a very great extent. Second, consider a situation where the first generation's C (C_0) is more than adequate to meet basic survival needs. Suppose the society decides to increase its saving by a tiny amount, cutting C_0. This would increase both saving and consumption in the next period, even if by a very tiny amount. When added over an infinite time horizon, there would be an infinite increase in consumption, which makes the result unstable. Both these features can be avoided if one uses a discount rate, however small, with a minor change in the Ramsey formulation. At the same time, we have argued that there is a practical justification for adopting a rate of discount to solve the intergenerational wellbeing problem. Koopmans (1960, 1965) incorporated the discount rate into the Ramsey model by taking a positive rate of discount.[4] His result continues to exhibit ethical congruency, and the required rate of initial saving would be much smaller than in the original Ramsey solution.

On the basis of the dynamic results of the Ramsey–Koopmans formulation, we can identify a condition for sustainable development in terms of intergenerational wellbeing. Now it is easy to realize that each generation must inherit a non-decreasing stock of productive assets from which it can create alternative states of affairs from which the intergenerational wellbeing of the next generation can be at least as big as the current generation's. Hence, we can claim that development would be sustainable if $V_{t+1} \geq V_t$ for all t. If one thinks that this is too strong a condition to hold for all future time, we might think of the responsibility of the current generation in terms of its own action so as to ensure $V_{t+1} \geq V_t$ at t. The

---

[4] Koopmans formulation of the problem would be Max. $V_t = \Sigma_t^\infty \beta^{(t-T)} U(C_T)$ for $t \geq 0$ where $\beta = 1/1+\delta$ and δ refers to the time preference of society, and β then becomes the discount factor.

latter is a weaker condition, but fairly realistic in terms of the current generation's decision-making.

The implications of V_{t+1} being greater than V_t are that, there would be several states of affairs (Cs) in the (t+1)th time period that are better than those in the tth time period. Some of these improved states of affairs could be the result of consuming part of the productive assets inherited by the (t + 1)th generation. These have to be eliminated because it would imply that the (t + 2)th generation would have difficulty in maintaining its intergenerational wellbeing V_{t+2} to be at least as big as V_{t+1}. Hence, a non-diminishing wellbeing (V) over time would have to imply a non-diminishing stock of productive assets or capital. Change in the stock of capital is the outcome of investment during a period of time. Hence, each generation must ensure non-negative investment for the sustainability condition to hold. Any net investment would result in an increase in productive assets for the next generation.

Genuine Investment

Productive assets are obviously of many different kinds, and the set keeps changing over time. For instance, it would include all human-made capital stock like machines and buildings. It would also include the whole gamut of knowledge and skills that human beings possess, often collectively referred to as human capital. Such capital would not only include scientific knowledge and technological capabilities, but the entire accumulated output of the human mind such as books of value and great art and music. Social institutions like democracy, judicial systems, maintenance of law and order, as well as social practices, which enhance and strengthen reciprocal social interactions or relationships of trust, are important as social capital, which contributes in a number of ways to economic productivity. Finally, we have renewable and non-renewable natural resources, biodiversity, ecosystem services, and basic life-support systems, which comprise natural capital. All of these make up the total stock of productive assets in a society. Positive investment would mean an increase in this total.

One challenge that arises in estimating the total amount of investment lies in assigning proper economic values to these assets. As is obvious from our description, many of them are non-quantifiable and most of them may not have markets from where a price could be observed. Also, market prices are typically a reflection of private costs and benefits, whereas the intergenerational wellbeing is a social concept. Society's valuation of a productive asset need not necessarily be the same as that thrown up as a price in a private market. A way out of this problem is to take the help of accounting prices of an asset, that is, the increment in social wellbeing resulting from a small increment in the stock of that asset (Little and Mirrless 1969, UNIDO 1972).

Social wealth, K, can be defined as the sum of all types of productive capital available in a time period, t, given as follows:

$$K_t = \Sigma_i\, p_{it} M_{it} + \Sigma_j\, h_{jt} H_{jt} + \Sigma_k\, r_{kt} S_{kt} + \Sigma_m\, q_{mt} Z_{mt}$$

where p, h, r, and q are the accounting prices for manmade capital, M, human capital H, social capital, S, and natural capital, Z, respectively. The subscripts i, j, k, and m refer to the number of assets in each category. Over time, the different types of capital could keep changing, some diminishing and some increasing. However, in the net, the sum of all types of capital, that is the social wealth must not decline to ensure sustainability. Mathematically, it can be proved that the rate of improvement in wellbeing is equal to the rate of change in social wealth (Dasgupta 2010). This is sometimes referred to as genuine investment.

In this chapter, we started with discussing the tensions between intragenerational and intergenerational inequity, arguing that while improvements in intragenerational equity is a necessary condition for sustainability, it is not a sufficient one. In addition, there is a need to make genuine investments for future generations. Is the matter really so simple? We explore the idea of genuine investments further in the next chapter, while continuing to explore the meaning of sustainability.

CHAPTER 5

Weak versus Strong Sustainability

Substitution Between Different Kinds of Capital Stock

From the last chapter, it is evident that genuine investment refers to a non-decreasing stock of social wealth across generations, where social wealth is the value of the net sum of different types of productive assets available to a generation at a given point of time. All productive assets are assumed to be equally important for social wellbeing, and because the sustainability condition only requires the net sum of the assets to be non-decreasing, it is assumed that one could be substituted for the other. Many economists like Solow (1993) and Dasgupta (2001) have argued that it is neither important nor feasible to bequeath exactly the same items of capital to the next generation. A particular capital may get exhausted or no longer be available. A new type of capital can become a substitute for the unavailable one, such that the flow of services from the stock of capita remains unchanged. This is quite obvious in the case of physical resources like fossil fuels or mineral ores, which could be depleted over time. For instance, if a generation uses up all fossil fuels, but leaves behind an alternative technological solution to provide all the services rendered by the fossil fuels, then there is no substantive loss for the next generation in terms of what they could potentially do. There is no reason why any particular species or a particular tract of forest should be preserved if their extinction creates other kinds of capital such as better urban spaces, or factories that could lead to an overall improvement in social wealth. Improvements in social wealth are taken as indicators of greater human wellbeing, maximizing which is the objective of sustainable development.

Economists like Solow have argued that this is the best that the current generation could do for the future. It would be impossible to know the future generation's tastes and preferences, as well as their needs and how they would choose to live. These would determine their wellbeing. However, if the current generation leaves behind the potential for the next generation to live as the current generation did, it would suffice from the point of view of sustainability. Sustainability is, in this sense, a concept that few would disagree with, yet find it difficult to operationalize through specific policy measures. Economists like Dasgupta (2001) have argued that the concept of accounting prices in arriving at social wellbeing incorporates the scarcity value of the different productive assets. For instance, a productive asset like a natural resource becoming very scarce would be indicated by its accounting price becoming infinitely large. Similarly, a pollutant, for instance, which would be considered an undesirable element in the determination of social welfare, would have a negative accounting price because an increase in its availability or incidence would reduce social welfare. These extreme movements of accounting prices would be signals to society to search for alternatives, or in the case of pollutants, measures to reduce them. It should be noted, however, that accounting prices are not actually observable like prices thrown up by the market, however distorted and imperfect they might be. In using either market prices or accounting prices, there have to be a lot of approximations made in estimating its value (see Chapter 6). What is theoretically the best could be quite different from what is estimated. Three broad approaches to valuing ecosystem services are discussed in Box 5.1. The preceding point of view, where all forms of capital are substitutable, at least to a very large degree, is referred to as weak sustainability.

A simpler and more direct way of looking at weak sustainability is a paradigm where we think of societies' utility as a function of consumption, the stock of renewable resources, and the flow of pollutants. While the first two contribute positively to utility, pollutants reduce it. One argument prevalent in the discussion of weak sustainability is in the following terms: if net investment is positive, the society's capacity to produce increases. Income potential increases, and hence, consumption may increase, leading to higher standards of living. Newer technologies ensure that renewable resources are maintained at a particular level while pollution is kept under control. Non-renewable resources are not taken explicitly, but are subsumed as inputs in the production of consumption goods. In such a situation, a positive net investment, that is,

Box 5.1 Approaches to valuing ecosystem services

There are three broad approaches to valuing ecosystem services, and the choice of approach is determined by the availability of data, nature of the ecosystem service, and existence of markets for the services.

Direct market valuation approaches use data from actual markets to estimate the cost incurred in recreating an ecosystem service artificially or through estimates of the contribution of ecosystem to the value added of a final commodity (production function). The cost-based approach includes the avoided cost method, replacement cost method, and mitigation or restored cost method, and is usually used when an ecosystem service needs to be regulated. The production function approach requires a good understanding of how an ecosystem service helps in the transformation to the final commodity.

In the revealed preference approach, individual choices are observed to discern their preferences. Here, first a surrogate market is identified for the chosen ecosystem service, and then, different forms of revealed preference methods are used to infer the value that a consumer attributes to the service. Some of the revealed preference approaches are the travel cost method and the hedonic pricing method.

Rather than using surrogate markets, markets may be simulated and values of ecosystem services can emerge from the interactions of agents in these markets. This is the stated preference approach that is usually used when one wants to make a change in the provision of an ecosystem service. Contingent valuation is an example of such an approach.

References

http://yourarticlelibrary.com/economics/environmental-economics/methods-used-for-the-environmental-valuation-with-diagram/39686/

http://earthmind.org/files/coed/01-5-1-ValuationMethods.pdf

economic growth itself will suffice for meeting the conditions of weak sustainability.[1]

---

[1] Suppose utility for society is represented as U(C, R, P) where C is the consumption, R is the stock of renewable resources, and P is the flow of pollutants. As income increases due to economic growth, C increases, R remains constant, and P decreases. Hence, maintaining weak sustainability $U_{t+1} \geq U_t$ is never a problem.

Given this line of thought, weak sustainability is about maintaining high levels of technological investments so as to ensure that there are enough manmade assets created so as to compensate for the loss of other assets. It is all about tradeoffs among assets, rather than choosing between them. Further, it is about identifying policy measures so as to improve the levels of human and social capital. In addition to the goods produced in an economy, there could be some undesirable by-products (often called bads) produced, represented by a negative accounting price.

Lasting pollution is a calculable oppression of future generations
—(Sen and Williams 1982, p. 346)

As the production of bads (like pollution) is inevitable, weak sustainability is also about determining how to compensate those adversely affected by the bads. Similarly, the implicit assumption of continued technological change and innovations underlies the possibility of substitution between different kinds of capital. It is difficult to predict the nature of technological change and innovation in advance, particularly in relation to the rate of change of depletion of a specific type of capital, for instance, oil. The future use (and hence the rate of depletion) of oil is unknown at present, but the possibility of slowing down of the use cannot be ruled out in the future. Hence, current policy measures would have to invest in possible substitutes of oil so as to reduce its future rate of depletion. At the same time, it should invest in technologies to reduce the dependence on oil at present.

There could be some assets, however, whose loss cannot be compensated for. Consider, for example, the extinction of a particular species of vultures, which would be represented by reduction in the quantum of natural assets concomitant with an increase in accounting price for the asset due to an increase in scarcity value (using shadow prices) for natural assets. This could have happened because agricultural productivity improved through claiming rich and fertile forest lands for additional production, resulting in a destruction of habitat for the vulture. No amount of manmade assets would compensate for the loss in wellbeing from this extinction. An obvious loss in wellbeing is the reduction in ecosystem services of scavenging. In addition, there could be a greater loss because it is not really known what benefits the existence of vultures has for the ecosystem and the biological cycle. It is known that, in the long run, extinction of too many species could cause an imbalance in earth's biogeochemical cycles, which could affect the welfare of humankind. Box 5.2 illustrates these issues by describing the gradual drying up of the

Box 5.2 The Aral Sea

The Aral Sea is located in Central Asia between Kazakhstan and Uzbekistan. Till the second half of the 20th century, it was the world's fourth biggest saline lake, fed by two rivers, Amu Dariya and Syr Dariya. In the 1960s, the then Soviet government undertook a major project to divert water from the two rivers to the plains of Kazakhstan, Uzbekistan, and Turkmenistan. This irrigation had a beneficial effect on the arid plains of the three countries, facilitating large-scale production of cotton and other crops. One effect of this agricultural growth was the severe damage done to the Aral Sea. Water levels began to go down remarkably, and the sea began to split into different lobes. In 1998, the water level had come down by 20 m from its level in 1960, and the volume of water had shrunk to about a fifth. Starved of fresh water, the salinity of the Aral Sea increased tenfold in around 40 years from the 1960s.

With the drying up of the Aral Sea, fisheries and communities that depended on them collapsed. The Aral Sea also received, as runoffs, water polluted with fertilizers and pesticides. The dust blowing from the lake bed was chemically polluted and became a public health hazard. The salty dust blew onto agricultural fields, degrading the soil. Croplands had to be cleansed with large doses of river water. Local climate change occurred with colder winters and hotter and drier summers.

In 2005, the southern part of the Aral Sea was judged to be irreversibly damaged. Kazakhstan built a dam between the northern and southern parts of the sea, ensuring that water flowing from the Syr Dariya flowed into and stayed in the northern Aral Sea. By 2006, water levels in parts of the northern lake witnessed small increases.

References

http://columbia.edu/~tmt2120/introduction.htm

https://earthobservatory.nasa.gov/Features/WorldOfChange/aral_sea.php

Aral Sea due to well-meaning human interference. These are the kinds of concerns that lead to another view on sustainability, strong sustainability, which is discussed in the next section.

The Special Role of Natural Capital

These issues had led to some economists and ecologists (Costanza and Daly 1987; Costanza 1991; Daly 1991) coming up with the notion of strong sustainability as an alternative view. There is a fundamental difference between natural capital and all other forms of capital in terms of the degree of substitutability. Hence, the approach to strong sustainability is about treating natural capital distinctly from the other forms of capital. In the approach to strong sustainability, there are two distinct interpretations of the role of natural capital. The first interpretation argues that all natural capital need not be preserved as it is as long as the value of the stock of natural capital does not diminish. This implies that there is no constraint or limit to substitution within natural capital (Neumayer 2000; 2003). For instance, this line of thought would suggest that one can use coal (a non-renewable resource) as long as the profits from selling of coal are invested in producing and promoting renewable energy resources. This interpretation has its own difficulties both in terms of estimating the value of a stock where market prices are not always available, as well as in the assumption of perfect substitutability within that stock. This interpretation assumes that no human-made capital can substitute for a non-reversible environmental degradation like a larger hole in the ozone layer. However, the reduction in natural capital represented by the hole can be compensated by any increase in other natural capital, say a rise in the number of butterflies.

The second interpretation argues that there are certain limits to substitutability, and there is some critical natural capital whose physical stock must be non-diminishing. For instance, one can think of some services from natural capital, which are made available in terms of flows. The rate of use of these flows ought not to exceed the regenerative capacity of that capital. To take an example, the erosion of top soil cannot be allowed to exceed the rate of formation of new soil due to weathering. The second interpretation implies two sets of rules to be adhered to for sustainable use of natural capital. First is that renewable resources should be harvested sustainably so as to make sure the stock does not decline. The second rule is that the pollution put into the environmental sink should not be at a rate greater than the natural absorptive capacity of the environment.

This interpretation addresses some of the more important aspects of strong sustainability as compared to the first one. For instance, it is known that a declining stock of natural capital may have adverse consequences, some of which could be observed or felt much later, but the effects and timing are not known with certainty. Hence, a good strategy for risk management could be to maintain their stock. It is also obvious that some natural capital provides basic life-support functions, and the loss of such capital would be irreversible at an enormous cost to human society. Discussions of strong sustainability lead us to an understanding that we cannot compensate the harm done to the natural environment just by doing an equivalent amount of good. This would be true from both the perspectives of inter- and intra-generational wellbeing. An initiative to install street lights resulting in the saving of two lives per day cannot be balanced out by shooting a person every day for violating a traffic law.

In the light of the discussion on weak and strong sustainability, two important issues emerge. The first is how to actually go about taking society onto a path of sustainable development. Which notion of sustainability is more pertinent? Which is easier to translate into feasible policies? The second issue pertains to the incomplete or inexact knowledge that science provides, when it comes to nature and ecosystems, or about the complete effects of pollution and wastes. Box 5.3 discusses Easter Island,

Box 5.3 Easter Island: The importance of natural capital

The story of Easter Island, a tiny 43-square-mile place 2,400 miles off the coast of South America on the Pacific Ocean is a well-known case of unsustainable development. The Polynesians came to the island around 1200 AD, and 500 years later, all human habitation had disappeared from it because of a lack of food. The Polynesians found a fertile place with plenty of coastal fish, palm trees, and birds. They cleared the land for agriculture. They cut down trees to make canoes for fishing and built a variety of statues, stone platforms, which depicted affluence and power. With economic prosperity, the population of Easter Island also grew.

Easter Island was a case where economic development through primary activities like farming and fishing and built cultural artifacts came at the cost of deforestation, overfishing, and reduction of soil fertility. The inevitable tradeoff between development and environmental conservation led to a gradual depletion of the stock of natural capital. This, in turn, led to a shortage of food. Social conflicts and hunger took its toll, and gradually, the human population declined to zero. All that remains of Easter Island are the statues that once stood erect on specially built platforms. Researchers believe that the environmental degradation was extensive, with deforestation leading to severe drought and soil erosion. Easter Island is a metaphor for sustainable development or the lack of it. The importance of conserving the stock of natural capital is made evident from this tale of environmental catastrophe.

References

https://soas.ac.uk/cedep-demos/000_P501_USD_K3736-Demo/unit1/page_14.htm

https://chrismaser.wordpress.com/2012/08/15/easter-island-a-lesson-in-over-population/

a poster child of environmental catastrophe as an outcome of a complete disregard for natural capital. If society has to prevent, or at least minimize future costs, then it has to come to a firm decision on a plan of action, based on imperfect knowledge of science, and an inexact idea about future states of affairs. It is to these issues we now turn.

Scientific Knowledge and Social Decisions

How then do we proceed in trying to move the world forward toward a more sustainable future? What would be the metrics to look out for? Which indicators are relevant and how should they be prioritized? As the sustainable development goals (SDGs) of assuring a minimally comfortable life for all humankind is in itself a distant reality, should that be prioritized over all else (United Nations 2017)? Knowledge about nature and the environment obviously comes from the physical and the natural sciences. What we need to do with that knowledge to achieve certain goals is a social decision. Hence, there is a need to blend societal and governance issues with the physical constraints posed by hard science. Conventional science, a classic example being Newtonian Physics, was dependent on mathematical precision, leading to perfect accuracy and predictability. This approach had influences beyond traditional science. For instance, conventional economics used the concept of static equilibrium from the natural sciences, which allowed precise predictions to be made about the allocation of resources facilitated by the invisible hand (Smith 1776/1976) of the market price system. Economics and other social science mimicked the scientific picture of reality, which reduced complex phenomena into their basic constituent elements making effective use of a paradigm suitable for controlled experimentation, abstract theorization, and quantification of all relevant variables.

The knowledge we have gained about nature, which comprise the biophysical and social systems, has made scientists realize that these systems are enormously complex and uncertain in a fundamental sense. Most natural problems can be described by situations where scientific facts are typically uncertain, the stakes of these uncertain outcomes are very high, and there are multiple ethical positions people might take on the issues. Finally, these problems are concomitant with the need for an urgent decision for managing the problem. Under these circumstances, the standard scientific paradigm discussed earlier would be found wanting and the predictions would be far from accurate. The traditional science of the 20th century had been expected to come up with hard facts and evidence, such that the inferences from those were both accurate and predictable. In dealing with the new kinds of complexities of natural biophysical and social systems, the previous scientific method seems to have been inverted. This critical inversion is sometimes referred to as post-normal science (Funtowicz and Ravetz 2003).

In this approach, scientific evidence is marked by complexity of a different kind, which cannot be reduced to its constituent elements. Even if the initial conditions are known and the process is deterministic, it is difficult to arrive at a final outcome or predict it even in a statistical sense. This is because a large number of outcomes are equally possible, and the system has several tipping points where its behavior changes drastically. Under these circumstances, where uncertainty and irreducibility are germane to the problem itself, the choice of an outcome, or trying to influence the outcome, would have to be based on an ethical decision, as there is no objective truth to choose from. Science, therefore, fails to offer a clear predictable truth. Hence, society will have to make a strict ethical choice in terms of the most preferred outcome.

> *All too often we must make hard policy decisions where our only scientific inputs are irremediably soft. The requirement for the sound science that is frequently invoked as necessary for rational policy decisions may affectively conceal value-loadings that determine research conclusions and policy recommendations. In these new circumstances, invoking 'truth' as the goal of science is a distraction, or even a diversion from real tasks.*
>
> —(Funtowicz and Ravetz 2003, p. 2)

In the context of our discussion, the issues of environment and sustainability are in the domain of science located in the world of nature. However, addressing these issues means we have to manage and adjust rather than become, as Descartes said, "masters and possessors of nature." Sustainability cannot be obtained by the invisible hand of the market, which is supposed to provide a system of correct prices. In the presence of externalities, prices have to be set through some contrived mechanism like contingent valuation. These are not correct, but rather corrected prices, set by some policymaker in a visible manner. On this, there could be public debates and differences of opinion, as well as conflicting visions, on what needs to be attained. Box 5.4 illustrates how the Maoris of New Zealand were able to curtail unsustainable practices by developing appropriate social practices.

Box 5.4 Sustainability through social norms: Learning from the Maoris

The Maori are the indigenous people of New Zealand. When the Maori, of Polynesian ancestry, first settled in New Zealand, they were overwhelmed by the abundance of food and natural resources. Unsustainable practices adopted by them at that time led to a shortage of food, as uncovered by archaeological evidence. Many large seals and birds had disappeared, forests were burnt down, and fishing grounds were polluted.

Over time, the Maoris's developed social practices to adapt to the challenges of depleting natural capital. This is evident from the belief that the Maori have regarding the interconnections of people, plants, animals, water, land, and air, representing a special life-force. The Maori have a myth regarding the creation of the world. The earth is regarded as the mother needing preservation, respect, and care. In this sense, the relationship of the Maori to nature is like that of a child to its parent.

There are five core belief systems that determine the impact of the actions of Maoris on the environment. The first concept is *mauri*, which is related to a core essence and life-force present in all natural resources and the environment. This *mauri* should not be altered too much. *Whanaungatanga*, participation and membership, is the second belief system that propounds that the Maori belong to the land, rather than the land belonging to them. Not only do they belong to the land, but they are one with it. They believe in the concept of belonging to the extent that they belong to their family, extended family, and even land and do not seek to possess anything. The third belief system is *whakapapa*, which is about relationships and connections. Everything in the universe is connected with each other. The connectedness of people with people is traditionally maintained through marriage and occupation. The social capital, thus, developed is useful in times of conflict. The fourth belief, called *mataurango*, is about understanding and clarity, which is useful in building a local community identity. *Mataurango* promotes the notion of a cultural heritage. The last perspective is *kaitiakitanga*, a traditional system of environmental guardianship. Practices of environmental sustainability, such as restricting overharvesting of exhaustible resources such as sea food or birds and treating natural resources as gifts for current and future generations, comprise different aspects of *kaitiakitanga*.

References

http://theoutlookforsomeday.net/assets/pdfs/The%20Outlook%20for%20Someday%20-%20A%20Maori%20Perspective%20on%20Sustainability.pdf

https://econation.co.nz/kaitiakitanga/

http://teara.govt.nz/en/conservation-a-history/page-2

Planetary Boundaries Framework

If hard science cannot provide the guidance as to how to determine criteria to define sustainability and throw light on the way forward, policymakers would be in a dilemma, as they need some basis for decision-making. A possible way out has been proposed by a group of researchers at the Stockholm Resilience Centre, where, instead of predicting different outcomes for the planet based on different input conditions, they have tried to identify certain key parameters that would be critical for the planet's continued wellbeing (Steffen et. al. 2015; Stockholm Resilience Centre 2017). These parameters would be crucial in determining the dynamics of the earth's system, that is, the integration of biophysical and human socioeconomic processes. These processes vary spatially, as well as over time. Human pressures on these processes can result in the crossing of some threshold (not known with precision) that would trigger sudden nonlinear changes on a continental or even planetary scale. There is also the possibility that many of these changes will be irreversible. Hence, the cost to humanity in particular and life in general would be extremely high. The proposed boundaries within which these processes must be contained are rough estimates surrounded by large uncertainties and knowledge gaps. Hence, managing these adverse outcomes (many of which are interrelated) require human intervention to decide on consciously staying well within the estimated limits. This, the research group has termed as the *safe operating zone* for humanity. The ethical choice is about the ability to stay within a desirable state of the earth's system in the face of anthropogenic interventions.

To summarize the major findings of this group, they identified nine major earth system processes, of which four have crossed safety limits into zones of uncertainty, namely, climate change, loss of biosphere integrity, land system change, and altered biogeochemical cycles. They estimated the climate change boundary at 350 parts per million (ppm) CO_2 equivalent.[2] In 2009, we were already at around 400 ppm (ibid). Similarly, the

---

[2] Climate change is caused by several gases and particles in the atmosphere. To arrive at a standardized way of measuring the potency of each of the pollutants toward climate change, all gases are converted to CO_2 equivalents based on their potency.

biodiversity loss boundary was estimated at 10 times the natural rate of extinction, but it was already as high as 100 to 1000 times the natural rate. With respect to the nitrogen cycle, the researchers posited that human activities convert 120 million tons of N_2 into reactive forms (for fertilizers and leguminous crops), which was in excess of what natural conversion processes break down. The other five processes are atmospheric aerosol loading, introduction of novel entities, global fresh water use, ocean acidification, and stratospheric ozone depletion. Of these, it is difficult to ascertain the planetary boundaries for atmospheric aerosol loading and introduction of novel entities (such as persistent organic pollutants) due to insufficient knowledge about the science related to their accumulation and transformation (ibid).

The findings of this group can provide some direction to policymakers in terms of setting and prioritizing their sustainability goals. These could include focused science and technology measures to address the immediate challenges and find cost-effective solutions. Most effective policy measures, however, would be those that could potentially affect all the parameters stressing planetary boundaries positively. Increasing awareness on sustainability-related issues and imparting quality education to all are examples of such all-encompassing policies. These would impact private decision-making positively. Decisions related to better management of global commons, that is, areas that are outside the political boundaries of any particular nation state, such as the oceans, would be far more contentious, as there could be multiple rival uses of the commons, and not all would agree on a socially optimum outcome.

To conclude our discussion on strong and weak sustainability, what clearly emerges is the need to take a trans-disciplinary approach to identify the challenges and keep the planet within safe limits where human development can continue to take place. In this context, weak sustainability is easier to handle at the policy level because any continued capital accumulation would lead to a sustainable outcome in terms of a non-diminishing capital stock. Strong sustainability conceptually offers a solution that is more likely to be conducive in keeping the nonlinear and complex earth's system in balance. However, on a practical front, this is difficult to manage because it necessitates looking after a much more diverse set of assets and ensuring that these are bequeathed to the next generation in non-diminishing quantities. The planetary boundary framework provides a way out of this difficulty by positing that the deterioration of certain sets of natural processes be kept within certain limits. This is consistent with the well-known precautionary principle of risk management, adopted by the United Nations. Sustainability research needs to embed the findings from social sciences and the natural sciences (however incomplete) into a broad policy debate about available choices, risks involved, and what they might entail for human development.

CHAPTER 6

Measures and Indicators of Sustainability

Introduction

So far, we have discussed a number of conceptual issues of sustainable development and indicated some of the ambiguities and complexities that characterize the process. It is important that, despite these ambiguities and complexities, we should be able to find some indicators and measures that at least help us understand whether a community or a country or the entire world is moving in the right direction. Obviously, these indicators and measures must go beyond measuring the purely economic and be able to capture social and environmental aspects too. Broadly speaking, there are two different ways of looking at these indicators. The first approach is to look at it in terms of macro measures, such as green measures of gross domestic product or genuine savings, which will be elaborated upon later, that could be used for a country or aggregated across an entire planet. Alongside these macro measures, there are a number of micro indicators that look at more detailed aspects of human nature interactions, looking at specific localized phenomena such as air pollution in a particular suburb in a city or the reduction of available groundwater in a well in a village. Alternatively, there is another set of measures that examine the adequacy or otherwise of the supply of natural resources to support a set of life-support activities for a particular species, referred to as the carrying capacity of the ecosystem. In a similar fashion, the impact on the environment of anthropogenic activities is often measured in terms of ecological footprint, which could be for a single individual, a specific economic activity or aggregated across a community of humans. Ecological footprint is a good indicator of the demand made by human activity on the natural resources, and hence reflects the stress created on the ecosystem. It also represents the choices humankind makes about consumption and lifestyles. Therefore, it is, relatively speaking, easier to take conscious decisions about ecological footprints. Box 6.1 discusses the extent to which the ecosystem is under pressure from high per capita energy use and its implications.

Box 6.1 Projected energy stress on Mother Earth as an outcome of development: The challenge ahead

Per capital energy use is frequently taken as a surrogate measure of the per capita stress on the planetary ecosystem. A simple projection of the stress on the ecosystem over the next century can be made using this measure. Taking 1990 as a base year and breaking up the global population into 20 percent rich and 80 percent poor, 1.2 billion rich people used, on an average, 7.5 kilowatts (KW) of power for a total of 9.0 tetra watts (TW) of energy. In comparison, the remaining 80 percent poor people (4.1 billion of them) were using 1 KW on average for a total of 4.1 TW. Hence, the total stress on the ecosystem was around 13.1 TW.

Now, let us assume that, at the end of the 21st century, the global population rises to 12 billion and the average consumption of energy for both the poor and the rich is at 7.5 KW per capita. In other words, we assume that the poor people have attained the standards of the rich people of 1990 through economic development, while the rich have maintained their consumption of energy constant at 1990 levels using better technology and other energy conservation measures. (To illustrate how conservative this estimate is, the per capita consumption of the average American at the turn of the century was 11.5 KW). With these assumptions, the total stress on the planetary ecosystem would rise sevenfold to be 90 TW!

To keep the environmental stress at 1990 levels, end of the century technology, production processes, and consumption patterns must be at least seven times more efficient. This is a huge challenge; at present, neither physicists nor engineers have an answer, and economists are yet to come up with a mechanism that would incentivize a sevenfold increase in technological performance in so short a time span.
Source: Daly and Goodland (1998).

In this chapter, we start by looking at the carrying capacity, followed by ecological footprint. The interaction of the supply of and demand for ecosystem services is captured in a concept called ecological overshoot, which is discussed next. We then talk of an alternate approach, where different economic, social, and ecological indicators are analyzed to understand the state of the earth. Depending on the sustainability objective, composite indicators can be developed. To conclude, we review a proposed framework for developing sets of sustainable development indicators proposed by an OECD taskforce.

Measuring Sustainability from the Supply Side: Carrying Capacity

An obvious question that must have crossed the reader's mind is whether there are too many people on our planet. This is especially true when we encounter crowded cities and congested roads. Even when not thinking of people, many might have wondered whether there was too much crowding inside a small pond or lake with many fish, amphibians, and water-plants, all depending on the resources available in the confines of the water body. A little reflection would tell us that there must be some physical maximum that the ecosystem of the pond can sustain. It could be the other way round too. One could think of an ecosystem where there was an abundance of resources that could accommodate more living beings within that system. In nature, very often, animals and even plants migrate to ecosystems with better resources if possible. The concept used by ecologists is that of carrying capacity of an ecosystem. It is formally defined as the population of a given species that can be supported indefinitely in a defined habitat, without permanently damaging the ecosystem upon which it is dependent (Arrow et al. 1996) (see Figure 6.1). Box 6.2 illustrates the carrying capacity as well as ecological footprints of select countries to demonstrate the wide variation across nations worldwide.

There are some problems with this particular definition. Ecosystems starting from very small localized ones to the entire earth cannot survive with one species alone. Nature, in this sense, is fundamentally interdependent. Hence, defining the carrying capacity in terms of one species can suppress the impact of this particular species on other species that share

ADDITIONS THROUGH DEMOGRAPHIC GROWTH

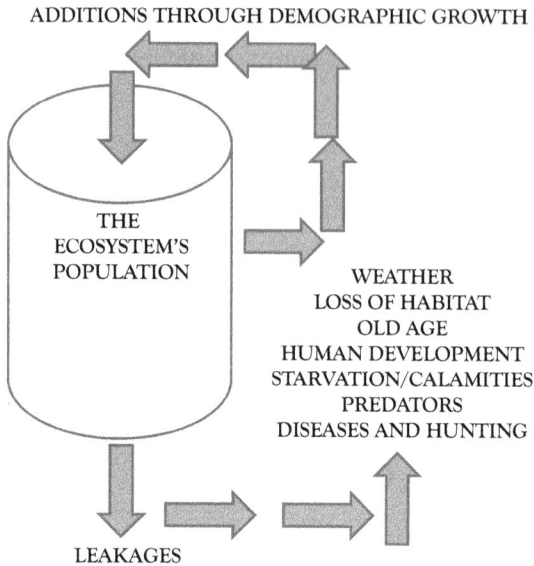

THE
ECOSYSTEM'S
POPULATION

WEATHER
LOSS OF HABITAT
OLD AGE
HUMAN DEVELOPMENT
STARVATION/CALAMITIES
PREDATORS
DISEASES AND HUNTING

LEAKAGES

Figure 6.1 Concept of carrying capacity

Box 6.2 Biocapacity: debtors and creditors

Depending on the relative endowment of natural resources and level of development, different countries can have different biocapacities and ecological footprints, respectively. Both the absolute value of eco-footprint and biocapacity and their per capita values are important to evaluate whether a particular country is contributing to the debt of biocapacity of the planetary ecosystem. In the table that follows, we provide some data for 2012 for select debtors and creditors of planetary biocapacity. For example, although the United States has a per capita biocapacity of 3.8 global hectares (ranked 25) because of its vast land resources, India has a lower ecological deficit because of its much lower ecological footprint of 0.5 global hectares per capita. While the numbers for Guyana look very promising, the reader must take into account its limited land mass and population, to infer that the implications for improving planetary biocapacity is limited. The reader must also note that four of the five countries listed as debtors of planetary biocapacity are also the four largest economies of the world in terms of GDP.

Country	Ecological reserves—the creditors				
	Ecological footprint per capita (in global hectares)	Ranking	Biocapacity per capita (in global hectares)	Ranking	Percentage that biocapacity exceeds ecological footprint
Guyana	3.1	60	66.6	1	2100
Brazil	3.1	59	9.1	14	190
Finland	5.9	15	13.4	6	130
Australia	9.3	2	16.6	3	78
Russia	5.7	20	6.8	18	19

Country	Ecological deficit—the debtors				
	Ecological footprint per capita (in global hectares)	Ranking	Biocapacity per capita (in global hectares)	Ranking	Percentage that ecological footprint exceeds biocapacity
Japan	5	30	0.7	112	600
China	3.4	52	0.9	101	260
South Africa	3.3	55	1.2	93	190
India	1.2	26	0.5	136	160
United States	8.2	3	3.8	25	120

Source: http://footprintnetwork.org/content/documents/ecological_footprint_nations/

the ecosystem. It is particularly inadequate for human beings because we can access distant ecosystems in different parts of the world with the help of technology and trade. We are not limited to consuming what is available in the local ecosystem we inhabit. Therefore, for human beings, the only meaningful measure of carrying capacity must be for the entire planet because it constitutes the ultimate boundary. Hence, human carrying capacity can be redefined as the maximum rate of resource consumption and waste discharge that can be sustained without impairing the functional integrity and productivity of the planet as an ecosystem with all its other forms of living species. Even in this definition, there could be

problems with the accuracy of estimates due to the fact that technological change can increase the carrying capacity (the same plot of land can
now grow more food than a hundred years ago) or consumption patterns
and lifestyles may change (we may decide to consume less or waste less)
(Arrow et al. 2004). Similarly, excess pollution could result in a decline in
the carrying capacity of the earth. At this stage, the reader would be keen
on knowing whether, with increased awareness and action, there has been
an improvement of bio-capacity globally. Box 6.3 discusses these trends.

Box 6.3 Trends in biocapacity

It is expected that more than 80 percent of the world's population will
live in cities by 2050. Thus, urban design will play a pivotal role in
reducing ecological footprint, which could be interpreted as a demand
on the ecological services from the city. Biocapacity, which represents the
supply of ecological services, can be enhanced in an urban area if urban-
ization is made compact and dense so as to free-up biologically productive land, which when left unharvested, can act as an ecological sink.

The future of world cities will determine to a large extent the success
of sustainability efforts to contain the planetary ecological footprint.
Better technologies and urban planning, now collectively known
as the smart city concept, can reduce the ecological footprint while
making cities more liveable at the same time. Many of these initiatives
revolve around increasing the population density of urban areas while
improving the public transportation options. A 100 people per square
mile increase in population density is associated with a 0.06 gha per
capita decrease in the ecological footprint. As urban infrastructure is
long lasting and influences resource needs for decades to come, infrastructure decisions make or break a city's future.

However, on the flipside, improvement in urban amenities is
also correlated with increasing affluence of its population, and hence
increased consumption expenditure. It has been found that a 1,000
dollar increase in expenditure, on average, correlates with a 0.09 gha
per capita increase in ecological footprint.

The trends in biocapacity, thus, remain uncertain.
Source: http://footprintnetwork.org/en/index.php/GFN/page/
footprint_for_cities/

It is little wonder that people who have made actual estimates of the carrying capacity have varied very widely in the numbers they have come up with. The estimates depend on assumptions made about technology and lifestyle changes. A lower standard of living for human beings (lower dependence on energy using technologies to save labor) would automatically result in a higher carrying capacity. The most conservative estimate has been two-three billion people, while the most liberal has been 1,000 billion people (Cohen 1997).

> ...carrying capacity is determined jointly by human choices and natural constraints. Consequently, the question, how many people can the Earth support, does not have a single numerical answer, now or ever. Human choices about the Earth's human carrying capacity are constrained by facts of nature which we understand poorly. So any estimates of human carrying capacity are only conditional on future human choices and natural events.
>
> —(Cohen 1997)

The largest number of estimates hover around 8 to 16 billion people. How exactly does one measure the carrying capacity? There are different estimation methods. A relatively easy way of doing it is to focus on one limiting factor, for instance, limiting food supply and its growth, and then estimating the maximum population that can be supported by the supply of food. Even in this method, there could be problems as to what could be considered as the minimal food requirements for a person, because it would vary considerably by age, health, gender, and social circumstance. In a similar vein, should we consider the absolute minimum food for survival for each person or would food be considered to be something more than a mere need for biological survival? A more sophisticated approach could be taking a set of limiting factors, such as food, water, and fuel supplies, and then trying to compute the carrying capacity. A little reflection will reveal that many of these limiting factors are actually interacting constraints. For instance, the availability of food is contingent on the use of fertilizers, which, in turn, could be constrained by the supply of fuel. On the other hand, the availability of a substitute for fuel could change the nature of the constraints substantially. Hence, the most sophisticated approach to measure biocapacity would be through a dynamic system of interactive constraints. It is imperative that estimating the upper limit of human population allows more room for interactive complexity and underlying uncertainties. Some well-known studies of dynamic systems (Forrester 1971; Meadows et al. 1972) have found that, under certain assumptions of technology and consumption patterns, the earth's economic system might stop growing from the reduced availability of resources, increased pollution levels, and continued population growth. The policy prescription would be to not only control population growth, but also to curb material consumption. There have been many debates about these estimates and prescriptions. Mainstream economists have been very vocal critics of this approach, reiterating that markets and price incentives would ensure reallocation of resources, technological innovations, and improved efficiency.

Not only does the measure of the carrying capacity differ, but also how different species approach the limits of the carrying capacity vary. Two different potential paths for species have been identified by ecologists, referred to as the K selection and the r selection. In the former, the growth rate of population at the initial stages when there is an abundance of life-supporting resources like food is very steep. As the availability of fixed resources becomes scarce, the population growth rate drops and the total population approaches the carrying capacity asymptotically[1] (See Figure 6.2). In the latter situation, the growth rate of population

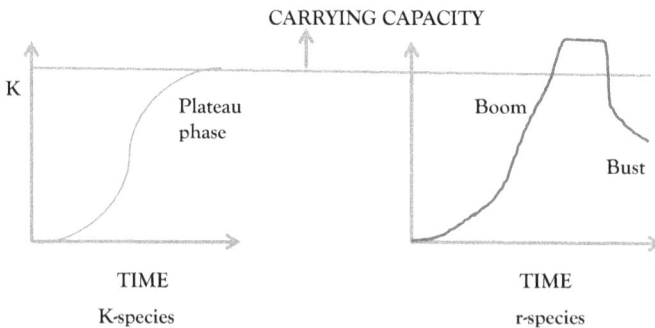

Figure 6.2 *Different population dynamics*

---

[1] The term asymptotically means approaching a value or curve arbitrarily closely (i.e., a limit is approached).

continues to rise at an increasing rate as long as there is some resource available, independent of the extent of scarcity of the resources. The growth rate may continue to rise at the same rate even after the available resources are exhausted. This, of course, cannot be sustained, and there is a sudden sharp drop in population, as deaths exceed births because of the unavailability of resources. If resources are renewed, then once population is small enough such that there is adequate availability of resources, then the growth rate may increase sharply again, resulting in a cyclical rise and fall of growth around the limits determined by the carrying capacity.

In our discussion so far, we have talked about the biophysical aspect of the carrying capacity of an ecosystem. Biologists point out that every species has its own rules of social behavior and minimal requirements of resource including space. This is easier to visualize in the context of human beings and their social systems. Different cultures have different conceptions of personal space, which depend not only on social norms and preferences, but also on incomes and availabilities. Hence, distinct from the biophysical carrying capacity, ecologists also talk about a social carrying capacity that tries to estimate the maximum population that can be sustained under different social systems. The social carrying capacity is usually substantially lower than the biophysical carrying capacity.

Measuring Sustainability from the Demand Side: Ecological Footprint

Initially proposed by Wackernagel and Rees (1995), the ecological footprint was adopted and popularized by Redefining Progress and the WWF (McLellan 2014). As the name suggests, the term ecological footprint refers to the imprint one leaves behind on the ecological environment as a result of one's economic and social activities. More specifically, it is a measure of the biological capacity of the earth that is demanded by a person, a population, or specific human activities such as production and consumption. In many ways, this is a better measure than the carrying capacity because it uses actual data that is not subject to uncertainties and other inaccuracies. The measure reflects our preferences and choices, and in this sense, it can easily be correlated with the environmental stress that our behavior creates. Also, it indicates how much of the earth's carrying capacity would remain for other species to thrive in, as humankind is just one of the many species sharing the same planet, and the greater demand humans make on the planet, the less ecosystem services are available for the rest.

One simple way of measuring the ecological footprint is to first find how much environmental space is available for a particular resource at a moment of time. The definition of environmental space is the global resource available at a moment of time divided by the global population at that same moment of time. It is a quick measure of the per capita availability of a resource (see Figure 6.3). To take an example, if there is a 100 acres of bioproductive land available at a moment of time and the total population is 50, then environmental space is 100/50, that is 2 acres per capita. Environmental space could be computed for a community, state, nation, or the world. This is useful because a country's consumption of some resource can then be compared with that of other countries quite easily and benchmarked along an accepted international norm. Policy prescriptions could also be generated from these measures. If the resource use or pollution created is more than the global average or an accepted norm, then one can follow conscious policies to reduce use. The converse, however, is not a good idea as the intent should always be to reduce the

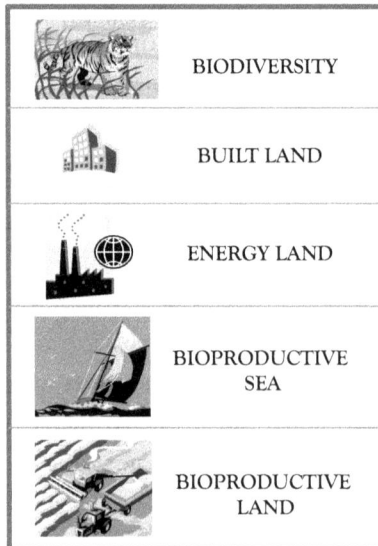

Figure 6.3 Constituents of the ecological footprint

ecological footprint so as to make available environmental space for other species. The concept is static in nature, in that it assumes a fixed set of technologies and unchanging human behavior.

Another measure to estimate the ecological footprint is using the concept of net primary productivity (NPP). All food and fiber, as well as mineral ores, come from nature. Food and fiber comprise renewable resources, and all food comes from plants using solar energy through photosynthesis. A common measure used by ecologists is net primary production, defined as the amount of plant material produced on earth, that is, the net amount of solar energy converted to plant organic matter. Another way of looking at NPP is the amount of energy obtained after subtracting the respiration of primary producers from the total amount of energy that is fixed biologically through photosynthesis. It is indeed the total food resource available on the earth for all species. The rate at which humans consume NPP is an important measure of the human impact on the functioning of the biosphere. The more we consume, the less is left for others in the food web. Various studies (Krausmann et al. 2013) have estimated that humans now appropriate anything from 24 to 32 percent of NPP for their own use. While the total appropriation is still not considered alarming, the growth rate of appropriation is approaching alarming limits. However, there is considerable concern over rising inter-regional variations in NPP.

The food web in which NPP is considered as the primary fuel operates in ways that human beings are not accustomed to thinking about. There is a famous example given by an American chemist, Miller (1971). He claimed that "300 trout are needed to support one man over one year. The trout in turn has to consume 90,000 frogs that must consume 27 million grasshoppers that live off 1000 tons of grass." This illustration indicates that the consumption of 300 trout actually requires far greater space than we normally suppose. It is evident also that, as a typical human being consumes many more things than mere trout, and the fact that human population has been growing quite rapidly in the recent past, the magnified impact of our food habits on the environment can be quite substantial, significantly higher than what we are accustomed to imagine.

Another measure that is commonly used is called IPAT (Ehrlich 1968). It provides a quick measure of the impact of human economic activities on the environment. This measure is particularly useful as a tool when we think of incremental changes. The formula I = PAT measures I, the environmental impact, which is the product of P, population, A, affluence and consumption, and T, the technology of resource use and waste. Population data is easy to obtain, but separate quantifiable data on technology or affluence is not easy to get. Hence, often A and T are clubbed together and measured in terms of per capita energy use. As an illustration, consider I = PAT in incremental terms. Suppose P doubles in the next 50 years and affluence (through economic growth) increases five-fold at current technologies. Then, I = PAT would be I = 2 × 5 × 1 = 10, that is, there would occur a tenfold rise in environmental impact. If we need to keep the environmental impact even at the current level, there has to be a tenfold reduction in resource use and waste creation! This would be quite a challenge for human ingenuity to come up with technological breakthroughs that would reduce resource use in the light of increasing population and increasing per capita energy demands. At the same time, this could be achieved through a change in consumption patterns, but lifestyle changes could pose an even greater challenge.

The simplicity in understanding the implications of the ecological foot-print has resulted in the development of several tools to measure individual footprints based on lifestyle choices (http://ecologicalfootprint.com/, http://footprint.wwf.org.uk/). The concept has further branched out into carbon and water footprints as well (McLellan 2014). However, there are several limitations of the measure of ecological footprint. To start with, as it is measured at a point of time, it does not embody the dynamism of technological progress or changes in consumption patterns. A time series of data on the ecological footprint can help circumvent this limitation. A comparison of ecological footprints across nations can provide an accurate overview of the spatial disparities in affluence and consumption patterns, which could help in better formulation of policies at a global level to reduce the overall ecological footprint for the global population.

Ecologists usually have in place some approximations of the regeneration rates of natural resources, and hence ecosystem services. The carrying capacity is an example of such a measure. A quick comparison of the ecological footprint with these measures provides an estimate of the extent to which humanity is using nature's resources faster than they can regenerate. This interaction between the demand and supply of ecosystem services is captured in a concept called ecological overshoot, which is discussed next. The enormity of the problem of ecological overshoot is evident from Boxes 6.4 and 6.5, which discuss the heinous impact of anthropogenic activity on the ocean ecosystem.

Box 6.4 The Great Pacific Garbage Patch

From the west coast of North America stretching up to Japan, there is a huge collection of marine debris, which is referred to as the Great Pacific Garbage Patch or the Pacific Trash Vortex. The ocean currents make the debris made of microplastics (formed from non-biodegradable plastic waste subject to photo degradation) spin and flow, resembling a cloudy soup. These debris move along the North Pacific Subtropical Convergence Zone north of Hawaii.

For instance, a Styrofoam cup thrown off the coast of California is likely to move south toward Mexico, then catch the north equatorial current and end up near the coast of Japan. The accumulation of plastics looks more like a soup than a regular dump, containing much larger items such as fishing gear in addition to microplastics. Scientists believe there could be larger and heavier debris at the bottom of the ocean as well, and estimate that 70 percent of marine debris sinks to the bottom.

Four-fifth of the waste in this patch originates from land-based activities in North America and Asia. The remaining one-fifth comes from marine vessels, offshore rigs, and large cargo ships. The bulk of the debris is fishing nets. Some more unusual items include computer monitors and even Lego toys. This waste can be dangerous to marine life in the vortex. Marine biologists have observed that some sea turtles mistake plastic bags for food. Seals and other marine mammals are considered to be at high risk because the plastic fishing nets serve as traps in which they get entangled. Marine food webs are also disturbed by the debris, as they block the sunlight from reaching the most vital autotrophs, namely, plankton and algae.

The breakdown of plastics through photodegradation is dangerous in two ways. First, they leach out polluting chemicals responsible for environmental and health problems. Second, plastics often absorb poisonous pollutants from the sea water, adversely affecting the food chain when consumed by marine life.

As the garbage patch is far away from any nation's coastline, no country would take the responsibility of organizing and funding its clean-up. One estimate suggests that it would take 67 ships a full year to clean-up a little less than 1 percent of the garbage there! Scientists agree that the long-term solution lies in eliminating the use of disposable plastics and increasing the use of biodegradable resources. Till then, the Great Pacific Garbage Patch serves as a constant reminder of the continuous increase of the ecological footprint of humankind, which compromises the biocapacity of the planet we live in.

Source: http://nationalgeographic.org/encyclopedia/great-pacific-garbage-patch/

Box 6.5 Dead zone in the Gulf of Mexico

A dead zone of an ocean or large water body is an area that is heavily deficient in dissolved oxygen (less than 2 parts per million). Dead zones are referred to as hypoxic areas, indicating the dearth of oxygen. There are many dead zones in the world such as the Baltic Sea, Black Sea, and areas off the coast of Oregon and the Chesapeake Bay. The Gulf of Mexico dead zone is the second largest one and covers up to 6,000 to 7,000 square miles between the inner continental shelf of the northern part of the Gulf of Mexico starting from the Mississippi river delta and stretching westward to the upper Texas coast.

The dead zone is caused by anthropogenic nutrient enrichment, particularly the elements nitrogen and phosphorus. These elements enter the upstream river water through runoffs of chemical fertilizers, soil erosion, animal excreta, and sewage. These elements, in turn, cause unlimited algae growth, referred to as algal blooms. As a result of this, the dissolved oxygen in the water is depleted, and the food chain adversely affected. Dead zones starve marine life, both because of the lack of oxygen and the presence of other toxins. The toxins are consumed by algae, and the algal bloom carcasses deteriorate in the water creating a vicious cycle. Massive fish kills, detected around the Gulf of Mexico, is linked to the hypoxic conditions.

Nitrogen and phosphorus originate from farming activities, and hence, their amounts vary with the farming season, leading to variations in the size of the dead zone as well. The situation can also be aggravated by natural calamities such as floods and hurricanes. The dead zone of the Gulf of Mexico has been estimated to reach the size of the state of Connecticut in 2016!

The Gulf of Mexico is a major source for the sea food industry. It supplies more that 70 percent of harvested shrimp, about two-thirds of harvested oysters, and around one-sixth of all commercial fish for the United States. As the hypoxic zone continues to worsen, the impact on fishermen's livelihoods and coastal economies would be adversely affected, as would the tourism industry.

Source: http://natural.news/2016-06-30-pollution-has-caused-the-dead-zone-in-the-gulf-of-mexico-to-expand-to-the-size-of-connecticut.html

http://serc.carleton.edu/microbelife/topics/deadzone/index.html

Ecological Overshoot

When humanity's ecological resource demand exceeds what nature can supply, an ecological overshoot is reached. It implies that we are essentially overdrawing resources at a rate faster than they can be replenished. This affects not only the quantum of resources, but also the flow of ecosystem services, as it interrupts biogeochemical cycles. Box 6.6 illustrates the extent of potential danger to the earth from overshoot using the concept of the Earth Overshoot Day. Looking at it more directly, overshoot would result in collapsing fisheries, species extinction, deforestation, loss of ground water, and carbon-induced climate change. Thus, overshoot is about the mismatch between the ecological footprint and carrying capacity, both of which can rise or fall. Here, the carrying capacity is looked at not in terms of the extent of human activity that can be supported, but in terms of biophysical capacity of resources. These resources include bioproductive land, bioproductive sea, energy land, built land, and biodiversity.

Box 6.6 *Earth Overshoot Day*

Earth Overshoot Day (EOD), previously known as Ecological Debt Day (EDD), is the date on which humanity's resource consumption for the year exceeds earth's capacity to regenerate those resources that year. Earth Overshoot Day is calculated by dividing the world biocapacity (the amount of natural resources generated by earth that year) by the world ecological footprint (humanity's consumption of earth's natural resources for that year) and multiplying by 365, the number of days in one Gregorian common calendar year

The following graph shows how, over the last 30 years, the overshoot date has progressively been arriving earlier. This implies that the fraction of the year taken to exhaust the earth's ecological services without impinging on its natural capital is becoming shorter. This also implies that we are gradually increasing the extent to which we are tapping into the ecological stock of capital. This can be correlated with the overuse of the planetary stock of natural capital, which implies that, at current rates of consumption, we would need a greater stock of ecological capital. This would need that we need more than one planet earth to be able to access the ecosystem services sustainably, without reducing the stock. The outcome of such an analysis is that, starting with one earth in the early 1980s, our current consumption already requires 1.7 planets. As that is, at the moment at least, an impossibility, the graph serves as a wakeup call for serious efforts from both the supply and demand side to reduce the extent of our ecological footprint.

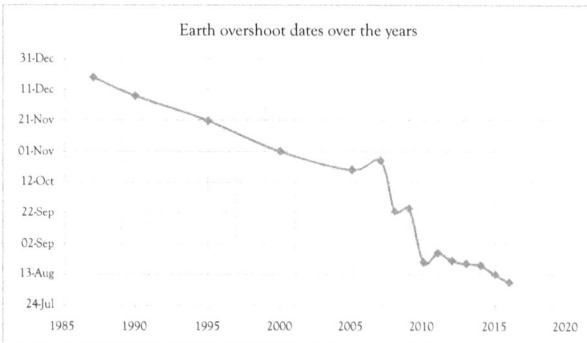

Progression of the dates of Earth Overshoot Day
Source: https://en.wikipedia.org/wiki/Ecological_Debt_Day

From these resources, we obtain food and fiber, as well as energy, and this is where we also release our wastes. Specifically, bioproductive land refers to the land requirement for production of crops and timber and for use as pasture. Bioproductive sea is the sea area providing fish and seafood for human and animal consumption. The land required to grow new forests to act as absorbers of CO_2 to offset the CO_2 generated from burning of fossil fuels for energy is referred to as energy land. Built land is land that is no longer bioproductive, as it houses buildings factories and other physical infrastructure. Biodiversity refers to the area of the land to be set aside to preserve biodiversity. The unit used to measure biocapacity is a productivity weighted average of biological capacity of different pieces of land in the world (or nation), called the global hectare (gha).

Data from the Living Planet Report 2014 demonstrates that the average ecological footprint per person worldwide was 2.6 gha. In 2010, the amount of productive land and sea area available (biocapacity) in the world per person was 1.7 gha. The amount by which humanity's footprint exceeds the planet's regenerative capacity is about 50 percent. If the world continues its business as usual mode, then, by the middle of the century, we would require two-and-a-half planets or more, depending on how high the standard of living becomes between now and then. On the other hand, it is obvious to live sustainably on one planet, humanity's footprint needs to come down dramatically within the next one or two decades. A stylized depiction of this is represented in Figure 6.4. This means that 1.4 earths would be required to regenerate humanity's current demand. We do know that national ecological footprints can vary largely.

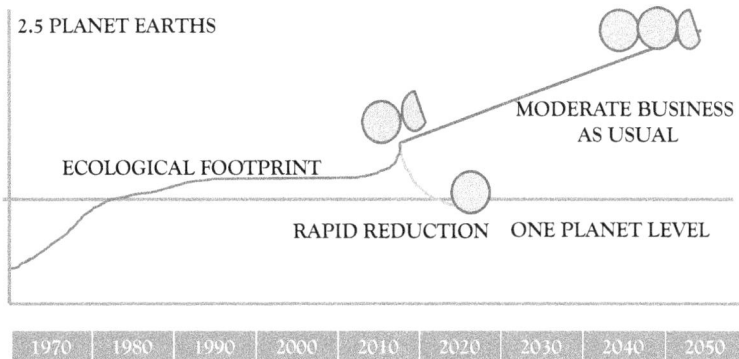

Figure 6.4 The number of earths needed to sustain humankind

Figure 6.5 If everyone in the world lived as they do in the United States it could require five and a half planets to live sustainably

The United States has the largest footprint, and if the rest of the world lived like the average American, we would need around 5.5 planet earths! (see Figure 6.5) The same report suggests that, compared to 1961, the global ecological footprint has increased by 2.5 times while the biocapacity available per person during the same period diminished by 50 percent. In 2010, out of humanity's total ecological footprint accounted for by CO_2 emissions (carbon footprint), the number of countries with a biocapacity deficit (that is where per capita ecological footprint exceeded per capita biocapacity) was 91 out of 152 countries. It was also noted that 85 percent of the global population lived in countries with a biocapacity deficit (McLellan 2014). This picture clearly reveals the rather alarming extent of ecological overshoot, and unless something is done urgently and decisively to change the situation, ecological disasters remain a distinct possibility.

Sustainability Indicators

Measures and indicators of sustainability are complicated for the simple reason that they must be able to indicate what damage is being done to the environment at present *along with* what it implies for future generations' opportunities. These opportunities, to be sustainable, must be similar to the ones the current generation is presented with. Broadly speaking, there are three sets of indicators, one set that is specific in nature such as pollution or the extent of degradation at local levels that can be aggregated over time or across space, but do not necessarily allow a composite understanding of the implications. The second set of indicators is composite in nature, which tries to compensate for the heterogeneity of the micro and specific indicators. The third set of indicators are macro or global in nature, which tries to accommodate, in a single measure, the state of sustainability of a nation or region of world. The extent of information conveyed by composite indices makes them useful, despite their other drawbacks.

As an example of a specific indicator, we could consider the measure of quality of water in inland water bodies. We would still need to know the benchmarks such as the tolerance limits for regeneration. There are a large number of such measures developed by many organizations, which cover a large variety of sustainability issues. For example, the European dashboard of sustainability indicators (Stiglitz, Sen, and Fitoussi 2009, p. 235) covers 10 different sustainability themes with 11 level-one indicators, 33 level-two indicators, and 78 indicators for level three. Level-two and level-three indicators cover 29 subthemes. Some of these indicators, like GDP are very global, whereas a measure of the percentage of smokers in a population is very specific, and they do not lend themselves to an immediate interpretation of their implication for sustainability. Such dashboard measures are difficult to use because of the extent of their heterogeneity. Nevertheless, they are useful in terms of their information content, and a follow-up strategy might require the development of more quantitative information so that it can inform policy formation and target setting. In a fundamental sense, sustainability is multidimensional, which implies more than one indicator is required to represent it.

However, parsimony is equally desirable. One way to circumvent the extreme heterogeneity of dashboards is to create composite indices (ibid, p. 237). Sometimes existing indices, such as the HDI, are scaled-up to include environmental issues, combining it with information on pollution, for example. Another well-known index, the Osberg and Sharpe (2002) Index of Economic Well Being (IEWB) measures consumption, sustainable accumulation, and social issues related to reducing inequalities and vulnerabilities. Such composite indices can also be inadequate as far as sustainability is concerned. For example, the IEWB focuses on social disparities for a particular generation. It falls short of measuring sustainability, both in the context of future generations and with respect to the availability of natural resources and ecosystem services. Over a period of time, it may be found that, in a country, there is an increasing divergence between GDP and IEWB measures. On the face of it, it might appear that there is a problem about sustainability of the economy. Yet, it could be entirely accounted for by a failure to reduce current economic inequalities. Any conclusion about the state of the natural environment would not follow from this measure.

Some other popular composite indices are the ESI, environmental sustainability index, and the EPI, environmental performance index (Esty et al. 2005). ESI covers five domains, namely, environmental systems, environmental stresses, human vulnerability, social and institutional capacity, and global stewardship (managing common environmental problems). This is a composite of 76 variables. EPI is a reduced form of ESI based on 16 outcome indicators, making it useful for policymakers to see whether targets are achieved. Here again, one problem remains in terms of the inability to indicate a norm or threshold value beyond which one could conclude that a particular country is on a unsustainable path.

Many years ago, Samuelson (1961) and Weitzman (1976) had argued that a correctly adjusted NNP, where all relevant depreciations of capital were accounted for, should equal the maximum level of sustainable consumption that can be reached for the present and for the future. The recently proposed, more fashionable, green NNP, which takes into account the consumption of natural capital, does provide a picture of how much of resources are used up in production, but does not actually tell us whether the level of consumption is unsustainable or not in itself. There is another important set of problems with green NNP with respect to the valuation of natural assets and their consumption. Market prices are either absent or are inaccurate estimates of true costs. Quite often, the methods of valuation that do not depend on market prices can be somewhat arbitrary where the valuation is extracted from a *what if* hypothetical kind of situation and considered to be speculative in nature by many accountants (Dasgupta 2001, 2009; Kolstad 2000).

Green NNP, despite all its measurement-related problems, is useful only to the extent that it indicates the amount of depletion of natural capital for the particular year. It does not tell us whether the society is over-consuming or under-investing in an unsustainable manner. This is a more dynamic question, the answer to which cannot be obtained by looking at a particular year's measure of green NNP. What it might help us in terms of policy measures is the knowledge of the kinds of natural capital being depleted and whether they are considered to be non-substitutable like biodiversity or other biogeochemical ecosystem services.

Another quite frequently used measure of sustainability for an entire economy is adjusted net savings (ANS), which relates to the changes in net wealth of the economy. This, in some sense, builds on the concept of green NNP, but in some sense, goes further in taking into account the stock of wealth (rather than the flow of national income). This particular measure was developed by the World Bank (Bolt, Matete, and Clemens 2002; Pearce, Hamilton, and Atkinson 1996) for almost all countries of the world. The measure is derived from standard national income accounts. Four types of adjustments are made to the estimates of gross national savings. First, the capital consumption of produced assets (depreciation) is deducted. Second, current expenditure on education (conventionally treated as consumption) is added to the savings figure. The third adjustment deducts the value of the depletion and extraction of natural capital. Finally, the country's CO_2 emissions, responsible for global pollution damage, are deducted. This country-wise measure is regularly computed and is readily available in the World Bank database. One observed limitation of this measure (when making comparison across countries) is that the first two adjustments account for the largest deviations across countries. Hence, differences in this measure across countries may not necessarily help us conclude that the one with the higher ANS is contributing to an improved ecological environment.

The discussion so far indicates the difficulty in obtaining a satisfactory aggregate measure of sustainability. In its absence, we may have to deal with imperfect measures, and there could be a large number of these, down to the local micro-level measures of environmental degradation. One reason why these measures remain unsatisfactory is the fact that measuring sustainability requires not only current statistically obtained observations, they need relatively accurate projections about the future. These projections will have to include technological and environmental trends, as well as trends in social institutions and political forces. There is also a need to look at the interaction between these two types of trends. Hence, such projections, especially the ones of social and political trends, entail specific answers to normative questions. Finally, sustainability is a global problem. It is not about assessing the position of each country as isolated entities. It is more about trying to look at the contribution each nation might be making to global sustainability.

Toward a Framework for Sustainability Indicators

To be effective in terms of information content, as well as providing adequate signals for policymaking, sustainability assessment would require both global measures along with well-identified dashboards of specific indicators. It is further desirable that the components of the dashboards should be interpretable as variations in the stocks of some assets. It is important to not only have a reasonably accurate valuation of these stocks, but also to have an understanding of critical thresholds of certain vital stocks, which would be in terms of physical measures. Indeed, there should be a subset of physical indicators, carefully chosen, on the environmental aspects of sustainability.

A conceptual framework for measuring and tracking sustainability was developed by the Joint UNECE/Eurostat/OECD Task Force on Measuring Sustainable Development (2013). The purpose of the framework was to pool together the different sets of indicators produced by national and international organizations. From this set, the task was to create a list of potential indicators, which would be based on one single conceptual framework and help in comparing and harmonizing different sets of indicators that are estimated around the world. The framework distinguished between three conceptual dimensions of human wellbeing. The first related to the present wellbeing of the generation in a particular country (referred to as the *here and now*). The second would be the wellbeing of future generations (referred to as *later*). Finally, there would be the wellbeing of people living in other countries (referred to as *elsewhere*). Thus, both the spatial and temporal aspects of sustainability are covered by the framework. Twenty subthemes, covering social environmental and economic aspects, have been identified, including subjective wellbeing, health and education, income, physical safety, trust, as well as energy sources, land, and ecosystems along with knowledge and financial capital.

Table 6.1 illustrates the 20 subthemes that were selected in developing the framework, as well as where they were relevant in the three dimensions discussed. For instance, land and ecosystems would be important for both the *here and now* and *elsewhere* because they are global in nature,

Table 6.1 Framework for measuring sustainable development: Relationship between the conceptual and thematic categorizations

Themes	Dimensions		
	Human wellbeing (*Here and now*)	Capital (*Later*)	Trans-boundary impacts (*Elsewhere*)
TH1 Subjective wellbeing	x		
TH2 Consumption and income	x		x
TH3 Nutrition	x		
TH4 Health	x	x	
TH5 Labor	x	x	x
TH6 Education	x	x	
TH7 Housing	x		
TH8 Leisure	x		
TH9 Physical safety	x		
TH10 Land and ecosystem	x	x	x
TH11 Water	x	x	x
TH12 Air quality	x	x	
TH13 Climate		x	x
TH14 Energy resources		x	x
TH15 Non-energy resources		x	x
TH16 Trust	x	x	
TH17 Institutions	x	x	x
TH18 Physical capital		x	x
TH19 Knowledge capital		x	x
TH20 Financial capital		x	x

Source: Adapted from UNECE/Eurostat/OECD (2013).

as well as relevant for *later* because sustainability concerns would require a minimum quality of this indicator. Themes like nutrition or leisure are only relevant for the *here and now*. They have no trans-boundary impact. The later availability of these would be determined by the accumulation of capital, which is considered as separate themes. The framework also goes into identifying how to measure the conceptual categories indicated. For instance, health in the *here and now* could be measured by life expectancy at birth. The same measure would also be valid for *later*. The corresponding policy indicators would include health expenditure, specific issues such as instances of prevalence of smoking, or suicide rates, or mortality, in addition to life expectancy. A smaller set of more specific indicators is provided in the framework for the same 20 themes. For instance, labor and education could be indicated by employment rate and educational attainment, respectively. Air quality could be determined by exposure to particulate matter, physical safety through death by assault or homicide rates. These, as is evident, would provide a small minimal set of indicators, which would give not only a quick immediate indication of some aspect of sustainability, but also allow a similar set of indicators from every country to be comparable.

In this chapter, we have provided a quick overview of the large variety of measures and indicators of sustainability. The measures may be inadequate or imperfect in many ways, but that is only to be expected. The inadequacy arises out of the difficulty in making projections of future trends, as there is a value judgment that needs to be exercised. The imperfections arise from the difficulty of measurability of the value of natural goods and services and the costs of environmental damage. Markets for these types of goods and services do not exist, which means that prices cannot be observed. We now turn our attention to why markets sometimes fail to account for all the social costs and benefits of human activities.

CHAPTER 7

Market Failures and Public Policy Interventions

In a market economy, goods and services are produced at a cost by the producer and sold to the consumer for a price. The good normally uses up resources such as raw material, labor, and technology, and they are all paid for. When the buyer buys the good, he or she pays the price to transfer the property right to himself or herself. Markets, therefore, function on the basis of prices and costs and are based on the concept of private property. Sometimes, in the making of a good, a by-product or waste may be created, which has adverse effects on people who are neither the producers nor consumers of the good. This third person, or society at large, has to pay a cost to mitigate the effect of the by-product, for example, toxic waste or a greenhouse gas. As a result of producing and consuming a *good*, society has to incur the cost of the pollutant, or a *bad* (opposite of good). We say the market fails in such a situation because the sum of the benefits that the producer and consumer derive does not account for the costs incurred by the affected third parties or society. On the other hand, there are instances of goods that are usually naturally available in abundance, which are owned by everybody and no private property rights exist, for instance, the air we breathe or the high seas. In such situations, there is no market for these goods defined by costs and prices, and there is a tendency to overuse the good, and hence leads to congestion or deterioration of the usefulness of the good. Both these situations create environmental stress. For instance, increased pollution in the first case and overfishing in the oceans in the second lead to such stress. Economists have developed a framework for correcting the failure of the market; in the first case to internalize total costs into the transaction, and the absence of property rights and markets in the latter case.

When markets are allowed to function by themselves without any governmental interventions but do not maximize social welfare,[1] they are said to *fail*. The failure could be due to several causes. It could be due to market power, that is, situations of monopoly or oligopoly-like market structures where prices charged are higher than the additional costs of production. Alternatively, market failure could result from situations where the market price does not adequately convey the actual costs of production or actual benefits from consumption, referred to as externalities. The former is a situation of a negative externality, and the latter that of a positive externality. Thirdly, market failure (or even the absence of markets) could result in situations when the good in question (say clean air) is non-excludable and non-rival in nature, which makes it difficult to extract value from people who consume the good. Fourth, information asymmetry and inadequacy of institutional support could be causes of market failure. For example, for a complete and well-functioning market to develop for electric cars, there is a need to have a network of charging points, which, if left to private players, could be grossly inadequate. The *network effects* could also be interpreted as positive externalities. In the sections that follow, we discuss externalities as market and institutional failures. We, then, discuss policy interventions to correct them and the challenges faced in implementing these.

Externalities: Effects and Policy Interventions

An externality arises when the prices, which are a result of the interaction of market demand and supply, do not adequately convey the actual impact of actions of either the producer or the consumer. A negative externality would arise when the costs of production do not take into account certain additional costs of production, because these do not have to be borne by the producer. Pollution from production of goods is an example; while the producer bears the cost of production, the costs of pollution

---

[1] This could be interpreted as the sum of the producer and consumer surpluses arising from arriving at an equilibrium price when the market functions perfectly. Consumer surplus is the difference between the total amount that consumers are willing and able to pay for a good or service and the total amount that they actually do. Producer surplus is the difference between the total amount that producers receive for a good or service (the price) and the amount they are willing to sell at.

(health costs, aesthetic costs, and costs of damage) are borne by society at large, and hence, these social costs are not reflected in the market price. Similarly, in the case of a positive externality, the demand curve does not adequately convey the total social benefit of consuming a good or service. Taking education services as an example, the demand curve captures the direct consumers benefit from the education, but fails to capture the additional benefits that education confers to society as a whole, because of the demeanor of the educated person or his or her problem-solving abilities, or his or her motivating someone to get an education that results in the person making a socially useful discovery.

The solution to addressing the problem of a negative externality, where the social cost (sum of private costs and externality cost) exceeds the production (or private) cost, is to internalize the social cost through fees or taxes or other measures. As a result, the costs to be borne by suppliers increase, all things remaining equal, this is accompanied by a concomitant rise in price and a fall in the quantity of the good traded in the market. It follows that, without any interventions, left to itself, the market would be trading in more goods than was warranted as compared to the socially optimum quantity. In such a situation, the market price would be lower than the socially optimum price. There would be a fall in optimal social welfare, which is why this is referred to as a market failure. The opposite would hold for positive externalities, but our focus on policy corrections would be toward negative externalities in the context of environmental pollution and sustainability.

Command and Control

The first approach toward internalizing externality[2] costs is referred to as *command and control*, where either a pollution limit or an emission tax

---

[2] Costs are normally assumed to be borne by the producer of a good or service. Inputs are purchased, or implicit costs are calculated in terms of opportunities foregone. However, sometimes, a producer does not pay for a cost that emerges out of production, which hurts a bystander or third party. For instance, a producer of aluminum emits smoke, which causes a lung disease in a person residing in the neighborhood of the factory. The cost of medical treatment is an external cost. Ideally, it should be internalized as a cost incurred by the aluminum producer. This is more efficient from a social point of view.

is imposed on a producer by the policymaker, typically a regulator. This optimal limit or fee is arrived at by equating the firm's marginal cost of reducing the pollution with the additional benefit that society would get as a result of the reduced pollution.

The pollution will need to be monitored, which may impose additional costs. There is a possibility for rent seeking also that arises because of the potential information asymmetry that can emerge between individual firms, monitoring agency, and the regulator (Kolstad 2000). Thus, there would result a certain amount of non-zero pollution that is optimal for each industry to produce, which is one critique of this approach by ecologists who are of the belief that optimal pollution levels should be zero. Further, this approach needs a lot of information to implement appropriately. The regulator needs to know the abatement cost functions of each firm at the micro level and arrive at an abatement cost curve for the industry. It is not in the self-interest of the firm to divulge the true information of its abatement costs to the regulator, given that the information would be the basis for imposition of a fee that would raise production costs. The regulator would also need to estimate the economic cost of all the damage caused by the pollution arising specifically from the industry. There are concerns with isolating the damage caused specifically by a pollutant emanating from a particular industry, identifying all kinds of damage that could be produced, and then, imputing an economic cost to the harm inflicted. Without this information, it would be difficult to arrive at an estimate of the marginal benefit that society would get as a result of the reduced pollution. Information intensity, therefore, is one serious drawback of the command and control scheme.

Another concern is that the marginal analysis results in local optima, that is, the choice of emission limit is appropriate at the micro level for the industry. However, in the context of sustainability, what matters is not the specific pollution emissions (flows) for an industry, but the impact of the sum total of the flows of all industries from all nations on the stock of the pollutant, and its interaction with other pollutants and their consequent impact on human and animal health and the ecology. There is no correlation with the global optimal pollution level and the local optimum pollution level arrived at using this marginal analysis, although the command and control solution is certainly an improvement as compared to leaving the market to function without any interventions.

Liability Rules

A second approach, where the challenge of information intensity is done away with, is the imposition of liability rules. Here, the firm is allowed to operate without any emission standards imposed on it, but with the caveat that, should the activities of the firm cause any harm to others, it is the responsibility of the firm to compensate the affected parties for the losses borne by them. Thus, in anticipation of potential claims of damage, the firm would have to set aside a certain amount of resources (create a liability fund), which would result in additional cost for the firm, once again internalizing the externality. As the firm would be best aware of the extent of damage its activities would be causing, it would be best placed to estimate the extent of the liability fund that it sets aside. Even this approach has its problems. First, there needs to be an efficiently functioning institutional and judicial infrastructure that would dispose of law suits fairly and quickly. Further, the *affected parties* must be empowered enough to claim their damages from the firm. These preconditions may not be met in several developing countries. Thirdly, it is almost impossible to isolate the cause of damage as a specific pollutant from a specific industry and firm. Under that circumstance, implementation of liability rules can lead to long-drawn lawsuits with no easy solutions emerging. Fourthly, the affected parties may be many, dispersed, and non-homogenous, and the costs of getting the parties together so as to make a claim itself may be prohibitively high. This is even more so if the affected parties are non-human sentient beings who have to be represented by special interest groups.

Property Rights

In both the approaches discussed so far, the role of the policymaker is paramount, whether as a regulator, or to keep the institutional mechanisms credible and objective. A third approach, suggested by Coase (1960), proposes that there would be no need of a policy intervention, and affected parties could come to a negotiated agreement with the producers of a negative externality if property rights were adequately defined, whether in favor of the affected party or in favor of the polluter, and the costs of bargaining were zero (frictionless bargaining). Property rights, assumed to be prerequisites for any economic good within a market system, are socially enforced constructs that determine how a resource or economic good is owned. They can be quite ambiguous for goods such as clean air or the high seas. This concept is best explained by a simple example.[3]

Consider a situation where there is a laundry located at the bank of a river downstream of a steel mill. The extent of effluent pollution from the steel mill is directly proportional to the production. Left to itself, the steel mill has no reason to install any sort of water filter to clean the effluent, it being most profitable to just dump it into the river. As a result, the output of the laundry, and hence profits, get adversely affected. The laundry can set up some sort of a water treatment plant, but this could impose a cost on the laundry. If we now assign property rights to either party (the right to pollute the water of the river or the right to clean water), we create a situation where the polluter and the affected party can negotiate with each other.

Let us first consider the case where the steel plant has the right to the water of the river (therefore the right to pollute it). In this situation, the laundry owner would weigh the costs (loss of profits) incurred by it as a result of unabated production by the steel mill with the additional profit it would make if the steel mill installed a filter. The owner would be willing to compensate the steel mill to the extent of the additional profits if it were to install a filter. There is, thus, scope for negotiation, and a possibility of a socially optimal solution (acceptable to both the steel mill and laundry owner, considered to be society) to emerge. Alternatively, if the property right for the river is assigned to the laundry owner, he or she would have the right to clean water. Hence, the steel mill would weigh the costs of installing a filter versus the net benefits for the laundry owner from installing a water treatment plant on his or her own. Depending on the cheaper option, the steel mill can then bargain with the laundry to implement the most cost-effective option so as to maximize the profit of the laundry owner. Whether the property right is with the steel mill or the laundry, the net outcome in terms of the extent of pollution reduction will turn out to be exactly the same, although the entity that possesses the property right will benefit more.

---

[3] Draws heavily for Kolstad (2000).

The Coasean approach has been used by many to justify a laissez faire approach toward governance. However, this is not appropriate as the fundamental assumption underlying the use of property rights as a mechanism for correcting externalities is frictionless bargaining, which is impractical.

Tradable Permits

The last approach is to create markets for non-tradable goods (or bads), such as pollution, to correct the market failures due to externalities (See Box 7.1). Thus, if a power plant were emitting CO_2 equivalents as an

Box 7.1 Creating a market for bads

The United States amended its Clean Air Act (CAA) to introduce a trading scheme for oxides of sulfur (SO_x) and oxides of nitrogen (NO_x), gases that were responsible for acid rain, a form of trans-boundary pollution. The CAA set limits for SO_x and NO_x from specified electric utility plants from the 48 mainland contiguous states of the United States. Each utility plant was required to obtain emission permits from the Environmental Protection Agency (EPA). Each permit allowed the holder a specified amount of emission, for instance, 1 ton of SO_x. The CAA also allowed these permits to be bought and sold in a market like any other commodity. This market would be an efficient allocator of emission permits according to the specific needs of each SO_x emitting unit, which could vary due to its vintage, technology, efficiency, and choice of inputs. Each firm would choose the number of permits to purchase or sell based on the marginal cost of reducing its emission and the prevailing price of permits in this market.

This is considered a *hybrid* program, as the government determines the maximum number of permits that can be traded in the market, but prices of the permits emerge from the market mechanism, independent of government interventions. The CAA does not treat the allowance to pollute (emission permits) as a property right. However, there have been some legal difficulties in defining the ownership of the allowances. If an allowance is not a property right, then can it be freely traded in the open market?

externality while generating power, one way to internalize the externality would be to restrict the amount of emissions from each plant by providing them a set number of permits to pollute. Generally, different power plants would have different levels of operating efficiency, and hence emission intensity, owing to the differences in technology, operations, management, and vintage. The permits would be tradable in nature, thus giving firms the flexibility to either reduce their own pollution or buy permits from cleaner firms who have permits to spare because of their abatement efforts. If the tradable permit market were operating efficiently, the price of the permit would be equal to the marginal cost of abatement of pollution for the firms, which would ensure that the pollution targets are reached at the minimum possible costs. This is a hybrid system, where markets are created artificially by the government, but allowed to operate independently to arrive at a price. The maximum quantity traded by the market, however, is defined by the government. Besides the economic efficiency that results as an outcome of using the market system, tradable permits are a potent form of policy because it defines the total pollution flow, which is arrived at from understanding the contribution of the flow to the stock of the pollutant and its effects on sustainability.

Non-Market Externalities and Policy Interventions

In many poor economies, there are a number of traditionally determined non-market transactions that also result in externalities creating divergence between private and social costs and benefits. Hence, externalities can be seen in a bigger sense as institutional failure. Poor societies are heavily dependent on ecological capital and the services flowing from them. Barring agricultural land, there are no adequately defined private property rights. It may be noted that property rights may not be at the individual or private level. A community or a state could have rights too. To illustrate this kind of externality, we will take the help of two simple examples; one which shows unidirectional externalities and the other is about reciprocal externalities.

Let us consider the case of unidirectional externalities. Consider a country that is rich in forest resources and the policymakers decide to export timber. The government grants a concession to a private firm to cut trees and sell abroad. Suppose the concession is granted for trees located in the upland forests of a watershed. It is well known that forests stabilize soil and water flow, while deforestation causes erosion and increased water supply fluctuation downstream. Suppose there are a number of poor farmers who are located downstream and become adversely affected by the felling of trees. How could the problem be resolved?

One possibility is that if the law recognized the property rights of the small farmers to ecological services of the watershed, then the timber farm would be compelled to compensate the farmers. There are practical difficulties, however. For instance, it could be that the damage done is located far away (in a big watershed) and the victims are scattered with unequal damages. Many of them may be unaware of the source of the damage. It is also likely that the timber firm may have more political clout in terms of being close to state officials who are supposed to monitor the forest. If no compensation occurs, the operating cost of the timber farm would be lower than the social cost of the activity. This gap would be larger if one goes beyond the short-term income effect on the farmers and looks at the long-run ecological damage done to the watershed. The macro outcome would also be unfair. Exports of timber would contain an implicit subsidy paid by poor farmers helping keep the price of timber low and benefitting the users of imported timber, who could be rich people in a developed economy.

This solution depends on the principle that the polluter pays. The sociopolitical conditions, however, may not be conducive to result in an actual compensation being paid. To complete the possibility, the right to fell trees could be given to the firm without any rights given to the farmers. In such a situation, the poor farmers would have to get together and compensate the timber firm to prevent them from felling trees. This is the converse—pollutee pays principle. From the efficiency point of view, both are equivalent, though the results are astonishing from the equity point of view. It may also be noted that, in such situations, the market for negotiation may be very thin if the poor farmers are not fully aware and organized.

In a poor country, as property rights are often ambiguous for grasslands, mangroves, coastal wetlands, and coral reefs, the state quite often treats it as public property, retaining its right to monitor the asset. These kinds of assets are often very difficult to monitor, and the information that the state may have could be inadequate for ensuring optimum use and conservation. The local residents, on the other hand, are much more aware of the nature of the ecosystem services, but there could be instances of the failure of collective action to ensure optimal use of common property resources (CPRs). In some of the ecosystems where outsiders may come as tourists to enjoy the aesthetic aspects of the ecosystems, there could be a way out in resolving the problem. The tourist could be charged and the proceeds could be distributed to local residents to maintain the natural ecosystem and ensure that garbage and congestion are limited.

Ecosystems are CPRs, and there is no guarantee that the state will take over its management. Take the example of common pastures or grazing lands in a village. To preserve the ecosystem's properties, overuse has to be prevented. If badly managed, free riders could easily degrade the resource. Hence, restricting the use in an equitable fashion may require some kind of charge or some social sanction for violating the collective agreement. In poor parts of the world, the importance of these CPRs is more than that in more affluent developed communities. These are often sources of food and incomes like community forests and coastal marine fisheries (Dasgupta 1993). Empirical estimates of these kinds of dependence measured in terms of income can be as high as 25 percent in rural India. In Zimbabwe, the poorest 20 percent earn 40 percent of their real income from ecosystems. Globally, it is estimated that 2.4 billion people depend on biomass for heating and cooking and 250 million poor people depend on coastal CPRs. In many of these CPRs, such as in a forest, private property rights are hard to enforce for a community because the benefits may not be homogenously distributed. The benefits could actually be mobile, like fish, birds, and insects, and any inorganic material of value may be non-uniformly distributed.

Most CPRs in poor economies are managed by local communities (See Box 7.2). The outcomes, however, are varied, ranging from obvious success to complete failures. Where a cooperative solution works, it helps create a network of working knowledge relationships, social capital, and trust. Cooperation also begets further cooperation, and the penalties for non-compliance become less harsh in societies that repose a lot of faith in cooperative solutions. Failure, on the other hand, is marked by community power structures that enforce entitlements based on wealth and influence.

Box 7.2 Trust and credibility as an alternative to prices

Sometimes, in a traditional (and often poor) community, property rights are not well defined, and hence, transactions are often not based on markets, but rather on certain social norms of trust and credibility. There is a literature that tries to look at grounds where promises are credible. A number of cases have been discussed, and there seems to exist a variety of reasons where transactions are possible in the absence of markets. For instance, mutual affection can be a basis for a credible promise, that is, both the parties care about each other sufficiently. The household is the best example of such promises. Promises could also be credible when it becomes common knowledge that those keeping their promises are trustworthy, and being trustworthy in a community context can be rewarding. People also have a disposition to recipro-cate in a similar fashion to people who are known to be trustworthy. A third reason could be where there is an incentive to renege on an oral contract, and mutual affection or pro-social disposition is not enough. In such situations, there would be a socially constructed mechanism for creating incentives not to renege.

The essence of the mechanism is that those failing to comply with agreements without any justifiable cause will suffer some penalty or punishment. Alternatively, if an explicit contract becomes necessary, then, of course, it has to be enforced by an established structure of power such as an administrative authority or court of law. In tradi-tional communities, these authorities could be tribal chieftains or warlords. Social scientists recognize that norms are often built on the strong emotional urge to punish those who have broken agreements. Formal markets may not be necessary for this purpose.

For instance, landlords would be preferred over landless, women could be excluded, and privileges become more and more entrenched. Lack of homogeneity in the community because of political or legal strife will also reduce the chances of arriving at a cooperative solution.

The management of most CPRs tends to change with the process of economic development. As incomes increase, the dependence on the CPR reduces breaking up the community norms, and hence degrading the ecosystem. Economic development can also lead to population stresses if the nature of the development is not enough to create new job opportunities outside the system, and cooperation could become fragile. In such situations, not all the stakeholders are affected uniformly. As cooperative solutions break down through the process of economic development, it becomes easier to enforce private property rights if people's dependence on these assets reduce and people themselves migrate out in search of better economic opportunities.

Prevalent Public Policy Interventions

While all countries today have formal laws and processes to address serious environmental problems, success in implementing them has not been as expected. One distinct difference between developed and developing countries has been the use in the former of economic incentives and market-based instruments to arrive at a social objective. Even under such market-based systems, rigorous checks and balances have to be built into the program to ensure compliance, credibility, and transparency (See Box 7.3). It should be unambiguously possible to measure whether a unit's emission is exceeding the number of permits it holds, and this information should be publicly available.

The experience of developed countries reveals the use of a number of regulatory alternatives to control for negative externalities like performance-based regulation, process-based regulation, co-regulation, economic instruments, use of guidelines and voluntary approaches, and finally, disseminating information and running public awareness campaigns on the importance of compliance. Performance-based regulations allow firms and individuals to choose the process by which they will meet the target set by law. Hence, the focus is on outputs, rather than inputs leading to government intervention being restricted to the output side alone. These regulations are typically used in the domains of health, safety and consumer protection. Many OECD countries have been increasingly using performance-based regulations in recent years. In process-based regulations, businesses have to manage production risks, implying that the producer must identify all the sources of hazards of its production process and develop least cost solutions to address these risks. It is believed that

Box 7.3 The ups and downs of carbon markets

Carbon emissions trading specifically targets the reduction of carbon dioxide (calculated in tons of carbon dioxide equivalent or tCO_2e) emissions using permits. The market was set in place by the Kyoto Protocol as a means to address the problems of climate change. The market uses multiple mechanisms of joint implementation (JI) and the clean development mechanism (CDM), which entails trading among developed countries and between developed and developing countries, respectively. In carbon markets, a country having more emissions of carbon is able to purchase the right to emit more, and the country having less emission trades the right to emit carbon to other countries.

From a peak of about 30 euros in 2005, the prices of carbon fell to 0.1 euro by 2007, owing to poor design and allocation of emission permits. This was followed by further volatility, related to business cycles, and uncertainty related to extending the provisions of the Kyoto Protocol. In August 2015, there were 39 national jurisdictions and 23 sub-national jurisdictions with carbon pricing instruments. There were 38 pricing instruments in use, which was a sharp increase (90 percent) from the 20 instruments prevailing in January 2012. However, such carbon markets cover only a small fraction of global greenhouse gas emissions. The total emissions covered are 7 gigatons (GTs) of CO_2 equivalents, which represents only 12 percent of the annual emissions of CO_2. Prices of carbon in such markets display a wide variation, ranging from 1 dollar to 130 dollars per ton of CO_2 equivalent. However, 85 percent of the emissions covered are priced at less than 10 dollars per ton. The monetary value of the instruments implemented is 50 billion dollars, as on August 2015.

Source: World Bank Report: http://worldbank.org/content/dam/World bank/document/Climate/State-and-Trend-Report-2015.pdf

firms are in a better position to do this, rather than being dictated to by a central regulatory authority. It is particularly useful in situations where ex-post testing of the product may be difficult or prohibitively expensive. Process-based regulations are widely used in the Netherlands, Mexico, and the United States.

Under co-regulation, the regulatory role is shared between the government and industry. Typically, a large proportion of industry participants formulate a code of practice in consultation with government. The code is enforced through sanctions imposed by the industry or professional organizations, rather than by the government. The advantage of this approach is that it allows industry to take the initiative in assuming responsibility for setting standards as well as compliance. It also leverages the expertise of industry participants more than the administrators. However, if left entirely to industry, it could lead to opportunistic behavior,[4] where industry would set standards lower than what would be desirable for maximizing social welfare. Regulators (for example, the National Competition Laws in Australia and the Netherlands) incorporate checks against the possibility of such opportunism.

Economic instruments like taxes, subsidies, and tradable permits are considered the best means of improving the alignment of prices with the objective of social welfare. These instruments have been used in a number of industries across many countries, such as, tradable permits in sulfur dioxide in the United States, green taxes in Denmark on CO_2 emissions, SO_2 emissions, and waste water discharge. Subsidies have been successfully in the Netherlands in the form of income tax deductions for commuting by public transport. In South Korea, firms that reduce pollution or recycle waste are provided long-term low interest loans.

Guidelines and voluntary approaches are not strictly enforceable, and hence are often referred to as quasi-regulations. In Denmark, they are used in the consumer protection industry. If significant non-compliance occurs, there could be court proceedings. Firms have an incentive to comply with these weakly enforceable guidelines because wide non-compliance should result in a far-stricter regulatory framework. Voluntary approaches are accepted by firms because this may help them pre-empt strict government regulations, and firms may also enhance their reputation by taking the initiative to do something socially useful.

---

[4] Opportunistic behavior occurs when, in an economic transaction, a party realizes that it can gain without paying—free riding on other people's efforts, or even plain cheating by deviating from the rules of the game. It creates distortions in economic results.

Enablers for Public Policy Interventions

Even where public institutions are strong, enforcing environmental and regulatory compliance is difficult because of the possibilities of opportunistic behavior, informational problems, market imperfections, and costs of measurement. There are some requirements for ensuring success for implementation of regulatory policies. For instance, markets may be far more complex than the textbook compliance of a regulatory firm. Thus, arriving at the correct figure for a standard or a tax can be a challenge. This leads us to the necessity of having a strong regulatory authority, transparent systems, and unambiguous regulations. Even determining the extent of tradable permits to be issued to each firm could be difficult, as could getting the firms to participate in the tradable permit markets. Getting such a constructed market to function would require norms and institutions, with possibilities for firms to take retaliatory action if a rival over-pollutes beyond the permits it owns or defaults on paying for permits. Thus, it is necessary to have a deep understanding of both markets and their functioning and an institutional infrastructure, which imparts credibility to constructed markets.

The economic agents involved in such types of markets and their associated transactions must have good skills in understanding and navigating the complexities involved. Sometimes, big industries take a long time to get down to the nitty gritty of trading of permits on a frequent basis. The sale and purchase of paper instruments in such types of markets represent an intangible property right for future collusion. Such transactions carry not only the usual commercial risk where a seller might default or a buyer go bankrupt, but also the possibility of false accounting. This necessitates the existence of a third-party referee with judicial powers to enforce the norms of the market. For these types of markets to work, it is imperative that the buyers and sellers keep their commitments. Moreover, the credibility of these markets depends to a large extent on the trust by the community at large because, in the final analysis, they are the ultimate beneficiaries. In developing countries, training and deploying of an adequate number of specialists for enforcing and monitoring environmental and social compliance is an additional enabler for public policy interventions to be successful.

CHAPTER 8

Corporate Strategies

In the previous chapter, we discussed how the policymakers and regulators might attempt to reduce pollution, or internalize unpaid social costs by affecting the behavior of business firms. In this chapter, we look at the same set of issues, but from the point of view of producers of goods and services, and how they might contribute to sustainable development.

For any process of development, business has a critical role to play, in conjunction with markets, government, and society. On one hand, business is responsible for creating demand for different goods and services through advertising and marketing, and thus can affect the consumption of resource-intensive products. On the other hand, production of goods and services can result in negative environmental externalities in the absence of government regulations or social sanctions that have been discussed in the previous chapter. Thus, business uses the (free or non-priced) natural resources as both a source (as raw material) and sink (to release wastes), and through promoting further consumption, can be responsible for an increasing rate of use of ecosystem services over time. There is a commonly held perception that for a firm to adopt a sustainable (environment and socially friendly) strategy, it has to incur a relatively high cost, in terms of current profitability. This tradeoff is often considered irreconcilable, arising out of a departure from business as usual. This need not be necessarily true, as is demonstrated in this chapter.

Here, we explore the different drivers of firm behavior in the context of sustainable development, given their constant interplay with regulatory institutions and other stakeholders. After discussing the different enablers that make a corporation go *green*, we examine the alternative strategies a typical firm may adopt toward this goal. This could include substituting raw materials, changing the production process, innovating to introduce new products, or managing the complete value chain of a service to minimize its environmental externalities. We then discuss the possibilities of *green-washing*, as there are large information asymmetries between different stakeholders and the firm. We conclude by trying to identify whether there are any key ingredients that can ensure that a firm behaves in a sustainable manner.

What Makes a Company Green?

Firms are often described as a nexus of contracts. They exist because of a complex set of explicit or implicit understandings among the owners of the firm, its employees, its suppliers, customers, competitors, investors, and several other institutions. Regulators, chambers of commerce, civil society organizations, the judiciary, and educational institutions are some of the key institutions that can affect corporate sustainability strategy. We examine the role of some of these stakeholders in influencing firm behavior, keeping in mind that, much like any other business strategy, sustainability strategy is viewed by the manager as a means of furthering her fiduciary responsibility to maximize shareholders' wealth.

Of the many drivers of corporate sustainability, the one that has been the most prominent historically has been government regulation and its enforcement. These include both prescriptive norms for minimizing pollution, providing a safe and healthy workplace, or to restrict discrimination of any form and market-based mechanisms to encourage environmentally responsible firm behavior. The nature of regulation, its stringency, efficiency of implementation, and changes in the approach of regulators over time are some of the parameters that affect how managers in a firm decide to manage the environment.

As discussed in the last chapter, regulations have evolved from being *command and control* to more market based, and regulators have started viewing businesses in a more collaborative role, setting standards and policy, as well as monitoring and inspection mechanisms in consultation with them. Hybrid systems of regulations combining elements of public regulation; government-supervised corporate self-regulation, mandatory information disclosure, and green procurement are being developed to promote the current trend of strategy toward sustainable development (Eisner 2004).

One of the key sustainability challenges for firms worldwide has been the availability of natural resources as inputs. Resource scarcity is becoming more and more acute as production levels increase. Firms respond to this challenge either by substituting away from scarce resources or by more efficient use of existing inputs and minimizing wastage. Not only does this make more business sense, but it also contributes to sustainable development reducing the pressure on the ecosystem. The other resource drivers for business are its suppliers, financers (including shareholders, investors, and banks), customers, and insurance firms. Linking sustainability attributes, such as good work practices and compliance to national regulations, to supplier and buyer relationships can reduce overall costs. It can also promote organizational learning as it is shared among partners, reduce environmental risk and liability, and provide cheaper financial resources for sustainable projects. The diffusion of learning and experience helps minimize adverse environmental and social impacts through process, product, and organizational changes. This diffusion constitutes a key benefit of developing good supply chain[1] relationships.

Risk management[2] can become a key driver of a firm's sustainability strategy, as was evident when consumers worldwide boycotted Nike when it was found that its suppliers were responsible for employing children who worked in poor conditions for unfair wages (Beder 2002). Insurance companies equate socially (gambling, for example) and environmentally risky (coal mining, for example) operations with increased financial risk and apply these criteria in their underwriting process. Sustainability considerations are used for business ratings of credit, customer, pricing, and investment for companies, which are, in turn, deployed by the financial industry to enable better risk profiling. Past practices and records of corporations are examined by banks along with the merits of the actual

---

[1] Supply chain in a production process is the network of vendors and activities that link the main production activity by providing inputs at the right time, at the right price, and having the right quality.

[2] Here, in the context of sustainable development, risk management means something more comprehensive than financial risk and its reduction. Risk could be many more sorts, many of them leading to large costs in the future, especially those that emerge out of environmental degradation.

proposal before approval of loans or other financing mechanisms for firms. Such pressures from the sources of capital that increase the cost of borrowing strike at the core of corporate decision-making.

Shareholders and investors are powerful change agents within the firm. The concept of socially responsible investing, starting with the formation of the Coalition for Environmentally Responsible Economies (CERES), which comprises investors who subscribe to a list of principles of environmental protection, has resulted in firms choosing their portfolios more cautiously. While CERES champions the use of investor voting to change corporate behavior, investment funds may influence behavior through moderating the flow of capital based on social and environmental criteria. Exclusions or negative screening refers to an investment strategy where certain companies or sectors are eliminated from the portfolio of industries to be considered for investment. These could include adult entertainment, gambling, nuclear power, tobacco, weapons, fossil fuel-based power generation firms, and mining firms with poor reputations.

Corporate strategy of a firm is influenced by customer demand and changing tastes and preferences along with information about current trends from consultants, trade associations, and even competitors. The effect of changing consumer preferences in favor of sustainable practices on business strategy can be quite complex. These effects can range from *green washing* (where firms project a sustainable image without actually doing anything) to business as usual (as consumers often do not pay a premium for products with sustainable attributes, although they claim they are willing to do so), to making actual changes in their activities to become more sustainable. The strategies adopted by the firm would depend on the extent of consumer awareness and its ability to convey to society its position on sustainability in a clear and credible manner. Of course, sustainable consumerism has led to the development and growth of new market segments such as organic foods and ecotourism. As with any other business strategy, the plans and actions of competitors could influence a firm's sustainability strategy so as to stay ahead of or at least keep pace with the competition. Firms compete over the extent of influence in changing the form and content of regulations depending on their state of preparedness and competence. Such influence may result in creation of barriers of entry for new firms and/or an unsustainable drain of resources for smaller competitors. Firms benchmark themselves against their competitors and are in constant search of improving the industry's best practice. Trade associations and consultants are conduits through which rules of thumb, standard operating procedures, and best industry practices are transferred among firms. By being the first mover or emerging as leader in setting standards and industry norms that other competitors seek to emulate, a firm benefits from a satisfied public (consumers and social stakeholders) and green investors while simultaneously putting pressure on competitors to catch up with it.

In today's connected world, the power of civil society organizations and media to mobilize social opinion and influence legislation is immense. In addition to legal consent to operate, firms also need *social consent*, for which close communication with social drivers, including the community is critical as part of a firm's sustainability strategy. Civil society organizations influence corporate operation directly or indirectly through diverse means including undertaking scientific research, conducting public protests, engaging in corporate alliances, influencing press coverage, and mobilizing public opinion. Of these, the pervasive effect of non-governmental organizations (NGOs) in changing societal norms and beliefs is probably the most potent and sustainable driver of superior environmental performance for firms, as it influences every firm employee, including senior management in the long run. Community and media have brought environmental issues to the fore of public and industrial concern informing and directing public debate.

Sustainability Strategies

Business strategies obviously aim to increase the long-term profitability and growth of a company, given the context in which it is operating. Sustainability strategies are very similar to business strategies, as they have a long-term focus, take into account current and future resource constraints and the business environment to steer the firm in a direction where it can improve its business operations. Thus, these strategies need to focus on either reducing costs or increasing revenues or both. Another set of strategies may focus on non-monetary business goals of a firm such as becoming a market leader, getting ahead of the competition or strengthening brands, the reputation effects of which also lead to increased long-term value of the firm. As environmental and social issues start occupying greater mind space of society, regulators, and consumers, firms will perforce be more concerned about weaving sustainability concerns into their business strategy.

A focus on sustainability could lead to the adoption of cost reduction strategies. The first approach in this context would be for the firm to embrace the concept of *eco-efficiency* and implement it. This would include a reduction in the material and energy used per unit of goods and services produced. Improved recyclability, reduced dispersion of toxic wastes, greater use of renewable content, and increased life cycle (in terms of durability) and service intensity (usefulness) of products are all features of eco-efficiency. Improving operational efficiency through process or product modifications could lead to reduced wastage, better output quality, and lower rejection rates, all of which contribute to falling costs of production. An indirect benefit from pursing eco-efficiency measures relates to better risk management, including better safety records, expedited permitting, and improved relations with regulators. A comprehensive corporate sustainability policy goes a long way in avoiding litigation, legal claims, and accident expenses (See Box 8.1). Further, such a policy, coupled with a strong reputation, results in reduced recruitment and retention costs, as employees are more willing to work in companies that are committed to social and environmental concerns. This allows the firms to attract the best and brightest potential employees, as well as to access new, local pools of labor. Improved employee morale can also result in greater productivity, thereby driving costs downward. Firms with strong reputations enjoy improved access to capital, as they are less prone to environmental and social risks, improving their creditworthiness. Further, with the advent of socially responsible investing and green financing, firms that are not focused on sustainability may face much higher costs of capital.

Strategies aimed at innovating products or processes as a response to sustainability challenges result in an expansion of the topline of a firm, as it identifies new markets and is able to charge a premium on prices for the additional sustainability attributes of its product or service. These strategies could use tools such as involving stakeholders to come up with

Box 8.1 *Enablers of sustainability strategies*

For a firm to engage in sustainability initiatives, there could be several enablers that have to come together. To start with, the power of human agency is paramount, whether it is in the form of managerial leadership or demands from stakeholders. Thus, in Alcoa, an aluminum-producing firm, a fifth of executive cash compensation is tied to safety, diversity, and environmental stewardship, which includes greenhouse gas (GHG) emission reductions and energy efficiency. Exelon, an energy-producing company, has introduced an innovative long-term performance share scheme that rewards executives for meeting non-financial performance goals, including safety targets, GHG emissions reduction targets and goals engaging stakeholders to help shape the company's public policy positions. PepsiCo identifies and discloses climate change, water scarcity, and public health issues as core sustainability challenges in its annual financial filings. GE attempts to integrate sustainability into the company's culture, ranging from hiring practices and training to employee wellbeing programs through its human resource department. The global water technology provider has both a sustainability steering committee and an enterprise risk committee. It identifies senior executives who are held accountable for sustainability performance.

Another enabler is to focus on one or two key initiatives and setting goals and roadmaps for them. For example, Coca-Cola has improved its efficiency of its water use by 20 percent, and is open to third-party evaluation of its water stewardship. Ford Motor Company and Walmart have focused on supply chain sustainability. PG&E's (autility company) environmental policy explicitly references habitat and species protection, and the company publicly reports detailed findings on its efforts. Adobe is using renewable energy technologies, including hydrogen fuel cells and solar arrays, and is also focused on reducing energy needs by improving the cooling efficiency of its data centers and *virtualizing* many of its systems, platforms, and devices to reduce GHG emissions. Bank of America has committed to increasing its portfolio of Leadership in Energy and Environmental Design (LEED) certified buildings, while Johnson and Johnson has focused on implementing a detailed policy that incorporates the Universal Declaration of Human Rights (UDHR), International Covenant on Civil and Political Rights, and International Covenant on Economic, Social, and Cultural Rights. It applies these principles not just in its overseas operations and supply chain, but also to all its workplaces.

Innovation in design and process using crowdsourcing is another way forward, as demonstrated by Nike. It has created the *making app* in 2013, where data on its materials sustainability is publicly available, enabling designers from the industry and beyond to design products with lower material and environmental impacts. Dell has been integrating alternative, recycled, and recyclable materials in its product and packaging design, improvements in energy efficiency, and design for end-of-life, and recyclability. Procter and Gamble has been developing and selling *sustainable innovation products*, that is, products that provide a greater than 10 percent reduction from previous or alternative versions in one or more of the following: energy use, water use, transportation, material used in packaging, and use of renewable energy or materials.

https://theguardian.com/sustainable-business/blog/best-practices-sustainability-us-corporations-ceres

new product or service ideas (crowdsourcing[3] is an instance), which, in addition to improving brand loyalty, also reduces the development costs of innovations. Many consumers take an organization's reputation and social contributions into account when making decisions to purchase its products.

As a key element of sustainability strategy revolves around building and nurturing relationships with stakeholders, sustainable firms have an improved ability to attract and build effective and efficient supply chain relationships (See Box 8.2). Profitable long-term business relationships are forged with partners across the value chain and the firm assists its partners in improving their production standards, thereby reducing risks

---

[3] Involving a very large number of contributors of money or other inputs into a project (paid or unpaid) usually mobilized through the Internet.

Box 8.2 Walmart: Leading with supply chain sustainability

Walmart started on its sustainability journey over a decade ago under the leadership of Lee Scott, the then CEO. Being a retailer, its focus was on supply chain sustainability, that is, the extent to which the procurement, manufacturing, and logistics departments within the company could directly impact sustainability targets. Their targets revolved around both environmental and social issues such as reduction of GHG emissions, waste reductions, more responsible hiring, and community development.

Through better routing and truck loading, driver training focused on minimizing idle time and progressive shifting, improved truck aerodynamics, fuel-efficient tires, and increased purchase of compressed natural gas powered trucks, they achieved an 84.2 percent improvement in fleet efficiency over the 2005 baseline by 2014. They also reduced the extent of the total waste generated.

The true success of Walmart is in influencing its suppliers (both small and large) to adopt more sustainable practices. For example, in 2007, Procter and Gamble agreed to start selling smaller, more concentrated bottles of detergent. This was good for fleet efficiency, good for the store (more shelf space for products), and reduced landfill waste. Walmart created a sustainability index scorecard through which they ranked their suppliers. They were able to create such scorecards for more than 700 categories of products. Attention was given in the area of sustainable chemicals to ensure that chemicals used in the products they sourced were not hazardous to humans.

Corporate responsibility may well go beyond considerations of direct profitability and core business goals. Walmart's efforts on economic and environmental sustainability would clearly give them a competitive advantage because they would be able to reduce costs. Contributing on the social front may not be profitable directly, but there would be goodwill generated by the company's contribution to the local community. Walmart committed 25 million dollars over five years to improve the communities' disaster response systems and gave over 2,800 scholarships for higher education to needy students.

A large company like Walmart would have a greater reach in the extended value chain in a manner that smaller companies would not.

> Hence, a large company achieving even a moderate improvement can have a significant ripple effect on the supply chain.
>
> *Source:* http://cdn.corporate.walmart.com/83/bf/f042060f46d-3b0e806289563c086/2016-grr-exectuive-summary.pdf
> http://scdigest.com/gsc/NEWS/15-04-30-1.php?cid=9251

for the partners, as well as itself. Further, improving the depth of engagement with consumers and society may result in an enhanced ability of the firm to better anticipate and understand trends to proactively plan for the longer term. This could be in the context of new regulations, heightened social expectations, and improved technologies. This enables the firm to strategically plan for the longer term, which, in turn, would result in increased revenue and market share. A proactive firm that has sustainability as one of its primary goals could also gain a first-mover advantage among its competitors by correctly anticipating and responding to social pressures.

Market Structure and Firm Sustainability

A firm's response to market and non-market pressures is mediated by the market structure it operates in. Thus, while a firm in a competitive market would be forced to match the moves of its competitors, just to stay in the reckoning, it has been shown that a monopolist may under produce quality of a product because of his or her focus on the marginal customer only. Most firms operate in an oligopolistic or monopolistic market where product differentiation is the key mechanism for them to make profits. Environmental and social attributes of a product or service can emerge as a key differentiator if the customer base is aware and has different willingness to pay for the product or service. Under these circumstances, it has been demonstrated that a set of firms are best off if they differentiate their product to the maximum. In other words, firms producing brown goods (that is, goods with very low environmental or social attributes) would always coexist with firms producing green goods, and the difference in sustainability attributes between the goods would be maximized for all firms to make profits. This could be of concern for society and provide a pointer for regulators, who would have to set the floor for environmental and social attributes to ensure that this tendency for differentiation does not result in a reduction of net economic benefits. The ability of customers to discern genuine sustainability measures from mere green-washing efforts can impact the extent of profits firm stand to make. Hence, encouraging disclosure of sustainability attributes and disseminating this information through measures such as transparent rating processes can lead to a *race to the top* for all firms within an oligopoly or monopolistically competitive market structure when there is a socially and environmentally aware customer base (Sarkar 2017).

The Emerging Role of Innovation in Sustainability Strategy

In the context of sustainability, a business firm's strategic innovation has to result in the creation of something new that enhances the firm's performance in social, environmental, and economic dimensions. While there can be a reduction in costs from becoming more resource- or energy-efficient, incorporating sustainability attributes into a product can result in additional revenues or in creating new or niche markets. As raising the bottom line or increasing the top line is the final objective of corporate innovation, the goals of achieving greater sustainability are aligned to the objective. There is debate regarding what constitutes an enhancement of performance. However, there is growing consensus that the innovation is not restricted to technology, but should also affect processes, operating procedures, business models, systems, and even thinking about the future (Szekely and Strebel 2012). Innovations for sustainability can be looked at in three distinct ways. They are incremental innovations, radical innovations, and systemic innovations that may be game changing.

Incremental innovation takes a particular view of a product or service where some new environmental social and economic issues are considered. Typically, such innovations tend to improve the eco-efficiency of the product or service. In most cases, such changes are add-on or end-of-pipe improvements in resource or energy use. Even when a new technology is used, it is often limited to a single factor of environmental performance such as CO_2 emission or use of water. These innovations usually lead to a reduction in production costs.

Radical innovations in sustainability are a bit more complex as they try to address how dynamic systems interact. Hence, these innovations would involve the analysis of separate parts with multiple interdependent wholes, feedback mechanisms, and nonlinear change. A typical instance of radical innovation would be the transformation of supply chains to make them more sustainable. Such innovations would not only call for a change in the products and services, but also in processes and operations. The innovations also impact labor conditions, workers health, and gender equity. Further, they would entail addressing environmental issues like where the raw materials came from, the wastes produced in the manufacturing process, as well as end-of-life impact (See Box 8.3).

Box 8.3 *How sustainability innovation works at Danone*

A key trigger to innovating for sustainability is presenting employees with new problems to solve and forcing them to think in terms of bigger frameworks and unconventional ways. This empowers employees to act, often producing creative outcomes that increase the firm's competitiveness. Danone, headquartered in Paris, one of the largest multinationals in the food sector, is a good example of a firm that practices this. According to the Danone leadership, no business plan is complete without a clear understanding of how it contributes to the world. Their CEO, Franck Ribaud's famous words "we cannot grow in the desert" reflects this understanding. The company's vision is to create economic value by creating social value. The sustainability strategy is loosely spelt out in terms of general guidelines and goals. However, each country's business unit and their employees are empowered and encouraged to implement these ideas into specific actions.

One example is their notion of the environmental platform, social platform, and the economic platform. The environmental platform's broad goal is to measure and monitor the carbon footprint of all its activities. The social platform focuses on the impact of all Danone activities on employees, as well as local communities where the people involved may have no direct connection with Danone. The economic platform goes beyond measuring tangible outcomes such as financial health or profitability into being concerned with intangible ones like reputation management. Danone had an internal reflection process around the question "What is the Danone we want for the next ten years." This reflection resulted in a decision to identify four equally important focus areas for the organization, namely, innovation, people, nature, and Danone for All. This entailed shifts in the company's central values, changes in its organizational structure, and encouraged internal debate from shared values to hiring practices, job descriptions, and employee objectives.

Danone, in involving its employees and tapping their innovative capabilities, floated a program called lab to land. The idea was to allow experimentation at a small scale and then facilitating the replication of successful projects at the country, regional, or global level. The scope of Danone's innovation process has been broadened in recent years to nurture and help radical innovations where the company's formal R&D unit has been allowed to engage with external parties through partnerships, joint ventures, and dialogs. It believes that technological innovation can come not only from the big companies that sell Danone machinery, but also from customers, people from the village, local suppliers, and so on.

Danone is an example of a company that, in determining its sustainability strategy and aligned innovative culture, has looked for other resources beyond its own. This includes collaborations with business partners and clients and public funding, thus making it part of a larger innovation ecosystem.

http://managementexchange.com/story/sustainability-innovation-strategy-how-sustainability-and-innovation-drive-each-other-and-comp

Finally, the game-changing (or systemic) innovations for a business firm relates to the transformation of relationships and interactions between the enterprises competing firms, customers' behavior, and lifestyle, and even the very objective of doing business especially the long-term goals. One example of such an innovation in the 21st century would be the sharing–borrowing–loaning economy, which has been described as the advent of the age of access or collaborative consumption. This has obviously been facilitated by the rise of information and communication technologies. The trend of collaborative consumption has the potential to significantly disrupt and change consumer markets where the use of the product, rather than the product itself is more important.

As customer preferences change, favoring products and services that address and solve broader societal and environmental issues, competitive advantage can be gained from innovations arising from sustainability as an objective.

Going Beyond Stakeholder Expectations of Sustainability

The most important driver of corporate sustainability is the business firm itself—the people working for it and the nature of the leadership. The significance of corporate culture is that it is autonomous in nature (not driven by external pressures of stakeholders, competitors, and regulators) and has the capability of looking ahead of the curve. Leadership plays a crucial role in influencing the culture of an organization to weave in sustainability concepts in every thought and action the firm takes.

Given its knowledge about its operations and their impact, the firm is in a far better position to understand the sustainability implications of any of its initiatives (See Box 8.4). At the same time, it is also best placed to balance different stakeholder expectations, as well as influence and shape them. The impact of the firm on molding change in consumer behavior, so as to restructure the nature of demand itself would be much stronger than moral strictures made by special interest groups such as NGOs, governments, or religious organizations. Sustainability issues have taken the proportions of crises such as climate change or social unrest, and firms are better placed to manage this change in the business environment than to government whose expertise lies in administering and maintaining status quo. Enlightened leadership within a firm, which has a time horizon far beyond the here and now can, therefore, play a critical role in designing corporate strategies that are sustainable, not only for the firm, but have an impact on the industry, which, in turn, through its value chain linkages, would lead to a more sustainable outcome for society too.

Box 8.4 *The sustainability balanced scorecard*

Sustainability initiatives in a firm are often viewed as additional to and often in conflict with the other business decisions of the firm. Yet, there is a need to align and integrate sustainability objectives with the day-to-day business objectives of the firm. One way to address this is to align sustainability measures with corporate strategies through a sustainability balanced scorecard (BSC).

A BSC is a framework that adds strategic non-financial performance measures to traditional financial metrics to give managers and executives a more balanced view of organizational performance. It typically reflects four interrelated perspectives of the firm: financial concerns, customer-related concerns, internal business processes, and mechanisms of learning and growth. Metrics are identified for each, which translate into goals that employees at all levels of the organization have to meet.

In addition to the aforementioned, a sustainability BSC would incorporate metrics related to environmental and social issues under each of the four broad perspectives. As these now become explicit objectives against which employee performance is evaluated, sustainability concerns become an integral part of firm strategy. An example of how some social and environmental concerns can be reflected within a BSC is shown as follows.

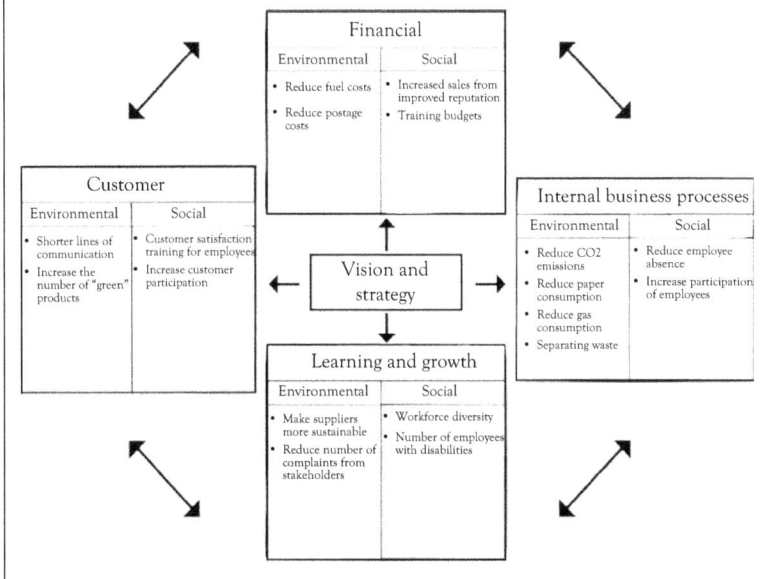

Through this, companies can delineate the relationship between sustainability objectives and outcomes with corporate strategy and profitability. By integrating sustainability measures into business practices and by clearly linking an organization's competitive strategy to its green outcomes, the BSC clarifies the relationship between sustainability outcomes and profitability or shareholder interests.

Figure from http://essay.utwente.nl/67287/1/boerrigter_BA_bms.pdf

We have discussed in the preceding two chapters how production and consumption can lead to market failures in the form of externalities. We have also discussed, briefly, how regulators and businesses grapple with the challenges of adverse negative externalities through the creation of pollution and wastes. Conventional economic wisdom creates solutions to the problems in terms of micro-firm or industry-based interventions. The macro or global impact of the problem is often not given due attention. Yet, arguably the biggest environmental challenge constraining the possibility of sustainable development is that of global warming and climate change. It has been referred to as the biggest market failure the world has ever seen (Stern 2006). The following chapter discusses the nature of the problem, the complexity of the challenge, and the difficulty of attaining a solution that has to be global in its impact.

CHAPTER 9

Climate Change as a Special Problem of Sustainable Development

Climate change, its causes and consequences, is arguably one of the most difficult problems facing humanity today. The roots of the difficulty lie in the nature of the problem itself and the inter-relationships it has with other many different branches of knowledge. The hard data regarding changes in climate and its implications comes from atmospheric physics, meteorology, physical and biological sciences, as well as ecology. The socioeconomic implications are identified through the disciplines of anthropology, sociology, and economics. Public policy and political theory is used for finding out possible global consensus on interventions to mitigate the problem, as any solution necessarily has to be global because the impact of climate change is not confined to any nation state, region, or geographical territory. Finally, philosophy and ethical reasoning are used to evaluate the moral worth of actions undertaken, which have an impact on not only the living generation of humans and other sentient beings, but also on all life in the indefinite future. Hence, the subject is complex and open to debate. Above all, as it deals with the future, uncertainty and ambiguity are germane to any discussion. Sometimes, such a problem is referred to by experts as a *wicked problem*[1] (Toman 2014).

Climate change represents a problem in, what is now referred to as, post-normal science (Funtowicz and Ravetz 2003). Post-normal science

---

[1] Wicked problems are a particular class of problems that are hard to solve for a number of reasons, such as fragmented knowledge and incomplete information, large number of people involved and the multiplicity of opinions, large economic costs of implementing a solution, and the complex interconnected nature of the different parts of the problem.

encompasses problems where the scientific evidence is hard to measure and interpret (see Chapter 5). There are different perspectives in terms of ethical positions about methods to solve the problem and the uncertainties are fundamental in the sense objective probability distributions cannot be used. Yet, the decisions that need to be made are urgent in the sense that a low likelihood outcome, if realized, could entail a staggering cost to all of humanity. If such a state of affairs is to be avoided, some action has to be taken in the present or at least in the immediate future. The imperfection and fuzziness of scientific knowledge is compounded by considerations of social values and ethical positions. These positions emerge out of debates that exist within the social sciences with vastly differing perspectives on social issues and required policy interventions.

The problem of climate change is an example of a system with interacting social and scientific subsystems that make forecasting difficult. Social action based on such predictions becomes deeply complicated and has feedback effects on the interacting subsystems that make up the representation of the problem. Solutions have to be arrived at through shared decision-making and public debate in at least two distinct dimensions. First, a solution must be acceptable to all of humanity, whether rich or poor, or belonging to an island state or living on a mountain. Second, the conversation between scientists and public policymakers must be transparent, with two-way interactions such that both groups fully comprehend the ramifications of a proposed solution from multiple points of view.

In this chapter, we will be talking about the nature of climate change and its implications for the economy, as well as for all sentient beings. We will also try to answer the question as to why climate change is likely to happen, and whether we should be concerned at all, particularly if the effects are likely to be long term. Next, we discuss that if some policy interventions are necessary, then what should be the nature of such interventions. Finally, the chapter concludes with a brief discussion on how policies are a challenge to implement to make them effective.

The Nature of Climate Change

Let us begin at a point where there seems to be minimum debate within the scientific community. There has been a significant rise in the volume

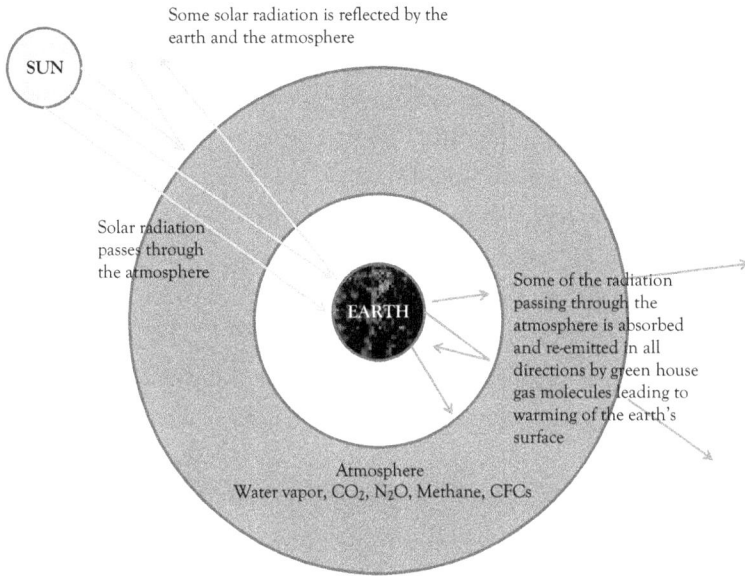

Figure 9.1 Schematic on climate change

of carbon dioxide and some other gases (collectively referred to as greenhouse gases, GHG[2]) in the earth's atmosphere during the last couple of centuries. There are obvious differences of opinion as to the exact volume and the rate of accumulation, but most scientists believe that the increase has been quite substantial when compared to the past history of humankind and the planet, as shown in Figure 9.1.

Given this fact, the next obvious question is why did this increase occur? The overwhelming majority of scientists now believe that the increase is essentially anthropogenic, that is, caused by human activities. It is patently evident from available data that the concentration of GHGs increased sharply and exponentially since the industrial revolution when the use of mechanical and electrical energy, with fossil fuels as their

---

[2] A greenhouse gas (GHG) is any gaseous compound (usually hydrocarbons) that persists in the atmosphere and is capable of absorbing infrared radiation, thereby trapping and holding heat in the atmosphere, leading to increased average global temperatures, referred to as global warming. GHGs are generally measured in CO_2 equivalents, based on their potency to trap and hold heat. Thus, methane is a CO_2 equivalent of 25 and nitrous oxide is a CO_2 equivalent of 298.

source, rose quite dramatically. The enormity of this rise is reported in Common and Stagl (2005), which suggests that there has been a fivefold increase in the per capita use of extra-somatic energy. The human body is like a machine that requires fuel from outside to be able to expend energy and work. This energy is called somatic energy.[3] The scientists involved in the project made heroic assumptions (admitting that the ability to work varies widely based on age, health, gender, climate, working conditions, and so on) to estimate the daily per capita somatic energy of a human being to be 10 MJ (mega joule) of work. This was defined as one human energy equivalent (HEE). By contrast, in the hunting gathering stage of human history, the HEE was estimated to be 2. Even the ancient hunters and gatherers had the assistance of tools such as bows and arrows and fire. At the end of the agricultural era and the beginning of the industrial one (around 200 years ago), the HEE was estimated to have risen to 4. This doubling was made possible with the help of work done by domesticated animals and the use of the wheel. The HEE for the beginning of the 21st century was estimated to be 19. The spurt in the use of energy came from mechanical and electrical energy sourced from fossil fuels such as oil, coal, and natural gas. During the same period, the world's population increased sevenfold from a little less than a billion to about 7 billion people. As the burning of fossil fuels along with certain agricultural practices emits carbon dioxide and other GHGs, the dramatic rise over 200 years is ascribed to this 35-fold (5 × 7) increase in energy use where emission of GHGs are a by-product. Hence, most scientists believe that the increase in CO_2 levels is due to anthropogenic causes (see Figure 9.2).

In this context, however, it may be noted that some scientists have doubts about whether the rise in GHGs in the earth's atmosphere is due to anthropogenic causes or not. They present evidence over long geological periods of time of cyclical changes in concentration of carbon dioxide in the earth's atmosphere, indicating that the changes may be part of those weather cycles. Other scientists are not convinced about the causal relationship between climate change and GHGs. Even though it is widely believed that the rise in GHGs leads to a rise in global temperatures, and

---

[3] The energy that can be expended by our own bodies without any external assistance.

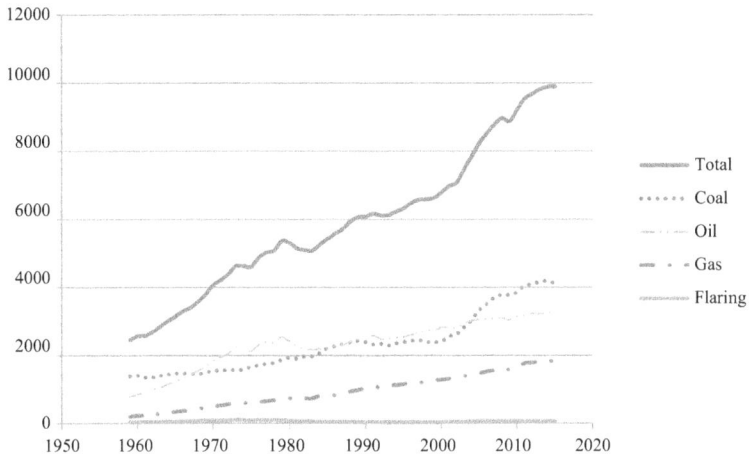

Figure 9.2 Global fossil fuel emissions by fuel type in million tonnes of carbon per year (MtC/yr)

Source: Boden, T.A., G. Marland, and R.J. Andres. 2016. Global, Regional, and National Fossil-Fuel CO_2 Emissions. Carbon Dioxide Information Analysis Center, Oak Ridge National Laboratory, U.S. Department of Energy, Oal Ridge, Tenn., U.S.A.

hence climate change, there are some who point out that the causality may be in the opposite direction: that a rise in temperature is leading to an increase in carbon dioxide in the atmosphere. Finally, there are some analysts who are not entirely convinced about whether there is an increasing trend in the earth's average temperature (Weisel 2013). The existence of natural causes such as weather cycles are not denied by mainstream scientists, who contend that such cycles may moderate or aggravate the anthropogenic effect on climate change.

Implications and Extent of Climate Change

If this is indeed anthropogenic, then what could be the implications of the rise in GHGs in the earth's atmosphere? This is yet another area where there are a lot of differences of opinion among scientists and social scientists. Some of the implications could be adverse, while a few could be beneficial. Biologists and ecologists talk about the impact of changed weather patterns on ecosystems, biodiversity, and agriculture, availability of food (See Box 9.1) and water, and human health. Social scientists express concern about the economic and political consequences of these

Box 9.1 *Climate change and food security*

The current practices of modern agriculture, often referred to as industrial agriculture, use enormous quantities of chemical fertilizers and pesticides. The practices are also extremely water-intensive, and large parts of the world's agriculture are still dependent on rain. These practices erode the nutritional quality of the top soil, and a lot of water is wasted through run-offs. Hence, there are long-term adverse implications of the business-as-usual model of agriculture. On top of this, the world population has been increasing dramatically along with rising incomes. Hence, the demand for food in terms of quantities as well as the demand for a different food basket is already exercising stress on productivity and availability. This situation is sometimes referred to as a food bubble, indicating that it is unsustainable in the long term.

If climate change occurs, then agriculture patterns are likely to be affected through changes in temperature, precipitation, volatility, pestilence, and other associated changes in the ecosystem. It is expected that climate change will definitely affect crop production in the tropical countries (the developing world) adversely, while the impact on northern latitudes is not that clear. For global food security, the severity and pace of climate change will be the critical factors to reckon with, rather than changes in the climate itself.

Goddard Institute of Space Studies (GISS) has a model for predicting changes in agricultural productivity and changes in geographical agricultural patterns. According to this model, there are two important conclusions that follow. First, global changes in temperature and precipitation during the next century are not likely to imperil food production for the world as a whole. Production of wheat and some other cereals along with processed food is likely to rise. On the other hand, productivity of non-grain crops is likely to decline. The pattern of changes is expected to be non-uniform, with, for instance, Pakistan likely to witness a 50 percent drop in crop yield, whereas corn production in Europe is likely to go up by 25 percent. The second result of the model is that crop yield and production would depend largely on the changes in the business-as-usual model. In other words, farmer adaptation will be a critical factor in how the effects of climate change on agriculture ultimately work out.

Most analysts believe that one impact of climate change on food security would be its effect on the poor, especially if they are environmental refugees.

Table 9.1 Trends in CO_2 emissions for select countries

Country or region	CO_2 emissions million tons (2004)	Emissions per person tons of CO_2 (2004)	CO_2 emissions million tons (2009)	Emissions per person tons of CO_2 (2009)	CO_2 emissions million tons (2014)	Emissions per person tons of CO_2 (2014)
United States	5,815	19.8	5,312	17.3	5,334	16.5
China	4,762	3.7	7,692	5.8	10,540	7.6
Russia	1,553	10.8	1,574	11.1	1,766	12.4
Japan	1,271	10.0	1,100	8.6	1,278	10.1
India	1,103	1.0	1,982	1.7	2,341	1.8
Germany	839	10.2	732	8.9	767	9.3
United Kingdom	542	9.1	475	7.6	415	6.5
France	386	6.2	357	5.5	323	5.0
WORLD	26,930	4.2	29,359	4.7	35,669	5.0

Source: selected from http://pbl.nl/sites/default/files/cms/publicaties/pbl-2015-trends-in-global-co_2-emissions_2015-report_01803.pdf

effects (IPCC 2014). Table 9.1 shows the trends in CO_2 emissions for select countries.

Weather scientists have made predictions using complex weather models of how weather patterns may change. As the weather models are complex and sensitive to the assumptions made, different models can come up with different predictions. (See Box 9.2) There will be many different kinds of effect of a change in climate. Some could be positive, such as a 2°C rise in temperature may improve the productivity of rice in the temperate zone of the world. However, a lack of water and the incidence

Box 9.2 Predicting climate through computational models

Climate models are extremely complex. For instance, a well-known model is developed and run by the Goddard Institute for Space Studies (GISS) in New York to make climate forecasts. It employs about 150 people who work on complicated algorithms that study and explain the behavior of the atmosphere, the oceans, the clouds, and vegetation, and they are all combined to provide results about the real world. This institute had made predictions, as early as in the 1980s, about global warming. The model divides the world into a series of 3,300 boxes covering the earth's surface area. There are 20 such stacks, vertically on top of the other, that cover the atmosphere, and the whole can be thought of as a gigantic cube made up of much smaller cubes. Time, in this model, moves ahead in half hour intervals, and for each instance, a new set of calculations are performed for each small cube. One complete run of the model simulates climate conditions over the next century. A single run of this complex model takes at least a month, even on a supercomputer.

There are over 20 different climate models that are in vogue today. In general, there is considerable confidence that climate models provide credible quantitative estimates of future climate change, particularly at continental scales and above. Over several decades of development, all the models have consistently provided a robust and unambiguous picture of significant climate warming in response to increasing GHGs. There are variations in the actual predicted outcomes of the models, even though the patterns of outcomes are similar. This is only to be expected as there are problems of estimation and approximation, and hence, these models are not free from errors and uncertainties.

Source: Kolbert (2006).

of drought could reduce productivity in the main rice-growing tropical areas of the world. In general, scientists believe that the negative effects will far outweigh the positive ones. One group of scientists has predicted slow moderate warming and that could give human societies enough time and resources to adapt to the new weather patterns. It would be relatively easy to assess economic impacts and determine how to take corrective actions. Another group of scientists haspredicted that extreme weather events may increase, such as unseasonal floods, unusual summers, or extremely harsh winters. The unpredictability of weather will increase, and this phenomenon is referred to as flickering. This is likely to happen as the earth would be seeking to settle into a new energy equilibrium. The unpredictability of weather would make adaptation very difficult, and economic impacts and corrective measures would be difficult to gauge. Finally, many scientists are concerned about the possibility of sudden and abrupt change in climate patterns. These are referred to as tipping points that trigger changes, which are not predictable from past patterns. Examples of such abrupt changes could be complete acidification of the oceans, shut down of ocean circulation systems, sudden release of methane from the Tundra, and the collapse of Greenland. The impacts would be catastrophic, with fewer resources available to mitigate them and no possibility of adaptation.

The rise in the average temperature is likely to have direct effects on economic output of the planet. There would be reduced water availability and much higher costs of energy, materials, and transportation. Agricultural productivity would decline, and physical capital and equipment would have to be replaced at accelerated rates to suit a changing climate. Some of the added risks of production would lead to higher insurance costs. Other kinds of risks, such as the increasing probability of natural calamities, would be non-insurable. At the individual level of human beings, the increased heat would lead to greater psychological stress, increased employee illness and absenteeism, and reduced labor productivity. Biologists have predicted that a rise in temperature would also increase the incidence of pathogens that could spread known diseases faster, and also result in the spreading of unknown diseases. Finally, the adverse effects of resource availability, health, and human habitat along with the rising temperature would have a telling effect on biodiversity, with increasing numbers of species likely to become extinct (Kolbert 2015).

If climate patterns change and the average temperature of the earth's surface rises by 4°C, then the polar icecaps might melt. If they do, then the level of water in the earth's oceans will rise. In that eventuality, the low-lying land would get submerged. One of the first areas to be affected would be south Bengal in India and parts of Bangladesh (the Sundarban region). This is among the most densely populated poor regions of the world. The rising sea level would threaten small island nations and dense coastal populations by destroying the coastal ecosystems and inundating low-lying areas. This would lead to many environmental refugees fleeing from the disaster-hit areas to inland areas, whose ecosystems would also be stressed because of other effects of climate change. Further, there could be political problems of giving them land, shelter, food, and jobs.

There are layers of uncertainty though.

> *For the last 10,000 years we have been living in a remarkably stable climate that has allowed human development to take place. In all that time, through the medieval warming and the Little Ice Age, there was only a variation of 1 degree Celsius. Now we see the potential for sudden changes of between 2 degrees and 6 degrees. We just don't know what the world is like at those temperatures. We are climbing rapidly out of mankind's safe zone into new territory, and we have no idea if we can live in it.*
>
> —Robert Corell

For instance, if we ask scientists what would be the magnitude of temperature increases due to global warming, their answer would range from anywhere between 2 to 6°C. This appears to be quite surprising if we consider that, on any day in any geographical space, the difference between the maximum and the minimum temperature is surely more than that. Seasonal variations in temperatures (say between summer and winter) are even bigger. Globally, the difference in temperatures between a very cold place like say Northern Canada and a hot place like the middle of the Sahara desert at mid-day would be more than 40°C. What then is the problem with a 2 to 6°C rise? Scientists are quick to point out that we are looking at variations and not the average. They are claiming that a rise in the average across the world is a completely different phenomenon compared with a routine variation in temperatures that we are so used to. Most scientists point out that over the past 10,000 years, the world has not seen more than a 1°C change in the average temperature. Climate has been very stable, where the human enterprise of agriculture flourished and settled styles of living were established. The new climate would be a zone of ignorance where the scientists are unaware of many possible changes, and are unsure how we will adapt to these and at what costs.

In trying to map the effects to causes triggered by global warming, scientists encounter deep uncertainty regarding the timeframe in which effects could take place, the incidence of the effects, and the costs they might entail. They can assign some likelihoods, but no scientist would be quite positive about their predictions. Long-term forecasts are notoriously difficult in areas where there is a lot of prior data. It is exasperatingly complex when one tries to predict events that have never happened before. Yet, most scientists would say that these events are likely to occur with a non-zero probability, and worse that most of the damages would be irreversible.

Why We Should Care

Given this state of uncertainty, it is difficult to think of a global consensus for action. The first problem is that there could be naysayers who might argue that if scientists are so unsure, there cannot be a very imminent problem, and hence, no action is warranted at all. There could be other people who, even if they agree that there might be some problems that emerge in the future, realize that it is unlikely to be discerned in their lifetimes. If the future is to be affected, then a strong selfish argument would be that why should we care about it and try to prevent it. Why should I pay for someone else's benefit in the future? This is more so when the beneficiary of ones sacrifice will be a person who will be born at a later date, and hence unseen and unknown.

This decision problem is essentially ethical in nature because it demands an answer to the question: what do we owe to future generations? This question is slightly different from the decisions a family or individual would make for their progeny. This is about all human beings living now taking a decision that might affect the future of all human beings to come (See Box 9.3). One way of trying to pin-down an obligation that the current generation may have is looking at the continuity of the human species and acknowledging the fact that our ancestors did leave us a world that was still inhabitable. Hence, there is an obligation

Box 9.3 Tick Tock Tick Tock…Is climate change announcing our doom?

The Doomsday Clock is an internationally recognized symbol that conveys how close we are to destroying our civilization with dangerous technologies of our own making. It started out with the concerns of a nuclear holocaust, but at present, emergent dangers, including climate-changing technologies, emerging biotechnologies, and cyber technology, are of equal concern. These could inflict irrevocable harm, whether by intention, miscalculation, or by accident, to our way of life and to the planet.

The clock first appeared on the cover of the Bulletin of the Atomic Scientists in 1947, to symbolize the urgency of nuclear dangers. At that time, it was set at seven min to midnight. It has since made an appearance many times, based on global nuclear events, for example, in 1969, as the Nuclear Non-Proliferation Treaty was signed, when it was set back by another 3 to 10 min to midnight. After a lot of back and forth, the clock was back at 10 min to midnight in 1990, as a consequence of the disintegration of Eastern Europe significantly diminishing the risks of nuclear war.

The concern for climate change was first reflected in the Doomsday Clock in 2007, when the time was brought forward to five min to midnight, on concerns of evident danger to humanity posed by it, such as damage to ecosystems, flooding, increased drought, and the melting of the polar icecaps. In 2015, the clock was brought forward to three min to midnight, because of: "Unchecked climate change, global nuclear weapons modernizations, and outsized nuclear weapons arsenals pose extraordinary and undeniable threats to the continued existence of humanity, and world leaders have failed to act with the speed or on the scale required to protect citizens from potential catastrophe. These failures of political leadership endanger every person on Earth." (http://thebulletin.org/timeline). Three min to midnight is the most severe alarm that has been raised till date, underlining the failure of collective action and consensus building to address the enormity of the climate change issue, although fears of nuclear war have reduced over the years.

Source: Bulletin of the Atomic Scientists (http://thebulletin.org/overview).

to leave a habitable world for the future. This world may be considered in the widest possible sense of containing not only human beings, but all sentient beings and living ecosystems. One might consider that, as the planet is not owned by human beings, we are merely stewards in charge of keeping it, or improving the condition in which we received it. This is a moral issue with practical implications[4] because people may have very different positions on it. Group consensus would be hard to come by and consensus at a regional, national, or global level would be even harder. Yet the problem of climate change would have to be addressed at the global level.

The Challenges

Because the source of the problem of climate change lies in the rising stock of GHGs in the atmosphere and global warming is directly correlated with the size of the stock, it is essential to restrict the size of the stock to an acceptable level where there is no temperature rise or the temperature rise is contained within a degree or two. Accepting the latter rise in temperature (1–2°C) implies that the current stock has already induced this change in temperature, and it would be nearly impossible to reduce the stock. Containing the stock at a particular level would imply reducing the flow emissions from the planet so that the increase in the stock dwindles over time and is contained eventually at a chosen steady level.

The first challenge, then, would be to choose a target stock of GHG, which could not be lower than the current level, but also is not too high so as to induce increases in temperature of over 2°C or more. It is also easy to observe that the lower the target stock chosen within this range, the more difficult and costly it would be for human economic systems to transit to a low (carbon) emission economy. On top of this challenge, there is the uncertain prediction that there could be tipping points where sudden catastrophic changes would occur if the stock exceeded a particular level. Predictions of tipping points also vary from model to model. Hence, the task of the economist or the global policy planner would be to choose a target that has three characteristics. First, it should be above the current

---

[4] See Chapters 4 and 11 for details of these implications.

level of stock; second, it should be below the lowest predicted tipping point; and third, it should be such that the costs of reducing emissions on planet Earth could be bearable and not too disruptive. The target cannot be too low, as that would imply a severe cut in emissions that could disrupt economic life and activity. If the cut is quite small, and hence, emission reductions are very moderate, there is a concern among scientists that, if the stock crosses a certain threshold, the changes in weather and climate could be nonlinear with a sudden break from past behavior, and which would be certainly non-incremental to economic growth. Alongside these thorny issues, there is the tricky question of simultaneously choosing the timeframe within which the target has to be achieved. This would determine the cost of transiting to low-carbon technologies. Given the state of scientific data on stocks and flows, there is no unique answer to these questions. The feasible set of stocks is large, the timeframes short or long, and on these depend the cost of transition.

Even if the target and the terminal date for transition were to be agreed upon, the time path could be different for different economies and there could be important monitoring concerns. What if a particular nation reneges on its share of solving the problem? For instance, emerging economies like India or China have claimed that, in their efforts to develop their economies and reduce poverty, there is an urgent necessity to make their societies more energy-intensive, while being energy-efficient at the same time. This could imply that, for these large economies, the time path could be first to increase GHG emissions for a decade or so before starting on the process of reduction. Yet, as the problem is global, there has to be a global consensus on each of the questions, which would be hard to come by.

Even if time paths are agreed upon globally for current action to be taken to reduce GHG emissions, there will be a number of difficulties that crop up in collectively sharing the costs of these interventions. Such interventions would include defensive investments to prevent future costs, like moving to use of renewable energy or even changing lifestyles. A strong argument that poor countries (with less use of energy and power, and hence with a lower contribution to the accumulated GHGs) often make is that, because the rich and more developed countries have actually contributed much more to the existing stock of GHG (even up to 80 percent according to some estimates), it is only fair that they contribute to the costs of mitigation in a proportionate manner. The developed economies have argued that the effort to reduce GHG emissions should be shared by all countries because it is the total carbon dioxide that matters, not where it came from. How should the costs be shared? Is there a fair way of sharing them where all might agree? The benefits from preventing climate change would be available for all (including people who are still unborn, and hence unknown) independent of nationality or economic status.

Finally, even if all these problems were to be resolved and some governable consensus was to be arrived at internationally, there would still be problems of policy design. How would specific nations ensure that economic agents—individuals, households, and business organizations—comply with their own targets as producers and as consumers? Should government use market incentives such as carbon credits and carbon markets? Or, should the governments fix targets for each unit and monitor them through what in the policy literature is referred to as the command and control method?

Policy Design

As there are no global institutions to enforce norms across nation states, any global consensus arrived at must be implemented and monitored at the country level. This can create problems of collective action failure because any nation might have an incentive to indulge in opportunistic behavior for short-term gains by reneging on the agreed consensus or worse still, monitoring agreed upon norms in a haphazard manner. Even before these concerns are addressed, there are differences in opinion among economists about the design of policy instruments to achieve a given objective.

The simplest and most potent sets of policy instruments[5] relate to prescribing specific emission limits for different levels of economic activity. An alternate approach is using price incentives to influence the economic activity so as to keep emissions under check. A hybrid alternative, where a market is artificially created for the reduction of emissions, by

---

[5] Discussed at length in Chapter 7.

issuing tradable emission permits to economic agents engaging in activities resulting in release of GHGs is also a policy option available.

The success of all national policy instruments is based on broad participation in mitigation efforts by all countries in the world. If there are countries that opt for less efficient policies, for example, allow voluntary reductions by some industries, or exempt large energy-intensive industries from the purview of emission reduction under the justification that those industries are essential for growth, then there is little that can be achieved toward reducing the threat of climate change globally. It is to this problem of cooperation or collective action that we now turn.

Collective Action Failure

The essence of the problem lies in the individuals, firms, or nations agreeing to incur some form of current cost, the returns on which will accrue in the distant future to an unborn generation, that is, the benefits will be shared by others who did not incur the cost. Typically, economic decisions are taken from a selfish and myopic point of view, and hence left to themselves; not many economic agents would be willing to incur such costs. This problem of collective action failure can be explained using a simple example, as discussed next.

Consider a community of n individuals, and each faces two distinct alternatives A and B. Assume that the individual is always better-off by doing A rather than B. For instance, A could be polluting and B could be not polluting by incurring some costs of reduction in emissions. Each individual when faced with the alternative where all do A, and another alternative where all do B, would prefer B. In other words, everyone would prefer to stay in a less polluting society, but no one in isolation would like to incur costs to do B. This is a generalized version of the well-known concept of prisoners' dilemma.[6]

---

[6] This refers to a situation in which two players each have two options whose outcome depends crucially on the simultaneous choice made by the other, often formulated in terms of two prisoners separately deciding whether to confess to a crime in game theory.

If decisions are taken by individuals in their self-interest (rationality), all would choose A, and the consequence would be the socially inferior outcome of a polluting society. This is referred to an atomistic result where each individual would do A, irrespective of what he or she believes other people might do. This implies the dominance of the individual's strategy. To ensure B as a social outcome, there has to be strict enforcement because it always pays the individual to renege on the social agreement to do B.

Consider another situation where everything remains the same, except that in the special case if an individual knows that everybody will choose B, then he or she will also choose B. In all other cases, the individual will choose A. The outcome need not be socially inferior if everybody chooses B. It also implies that the dominance of the individual strategy does not hold.

The former (a market outcome for instance) is referred to as the isolation paradox (see Chapter 3). The latter case is called the assurance problem (see Chapter 3). The real problem lies in ensuring that all do B. This could be assured by some strong social ethic where all are willing to make a sacrifice for the socially preferred outcome.

When there is a global problem that needs multilateral cooperation, which entails incurring costs to reduce carbon emissions in the present, to prevent a future catastrophe, arriving at a consensus is difficult. This is demonstrated by the several conference-of-parties after the Kyoto Protocol, discussed in the next chapter. It is even more difficult to ensure that countries adhere to their stated commitments, and there is no mechanism to enforce the agreed upon norms at the global level.

Conclusion

The problem of climate change has layers of complexity built into it. Action for a solution seems to be well-nigh impossible from the way we have posed the problem and argued the case. It is indeed true that the world has been trying without much success to arrive at a consensus, though everyone agrees that a solution is needed. There are statements made to the effect that, if we incur current costs to prevent future damage and the problem of climate change turns out to be not as severe as it is currently thought to be, we would have *bought* ourselves a cleaner, greener, and possibly healthier planet in the process (Stern 2008).

If a solution is so difficult and the matter so complex, why do we waste time on it at all? The crux of the matter lies in the recognition that solutions do exist and implementing them is necessary. Implementation may not be that difficult if a strong social and environmental ethic across individuals push nation states to act together toward a cooperative outcome. All of us as individuals could be convinced of the need to act in terms of changing our lifestyles and our consumption preferences. That would entail a commitment each one of us would have to make to our responsibility toward others, not only of people living in our own generation, but all those yet unborn and unknown.

CHAPTER 10

Sustainability and the International Political Economy

Introduction

After the brief discussion of the political economy of climate change in the previous chapter, we explore the international political economy of sustainability here. As sustainability cuts across national boundaries, arriving at any agreement on sustainability at a global level involves a deep understanding of entrenched power relations at all levels, ranging from interactions among nation states, to concerns about local and regional development and down to the micro scale of communities and households. Further, any agreements reached at a global level must be consistent with national priorities, policies, and initiatives to be effective. We will discuss the international political economy of sustainability from 1972 when the United Nations Conference on Human Environment was held at Stockholm. This conference is recognized as the first international effort to link human behavior and environmental issues in addressing environmental problems. Prior to this, there was a growing awareness about environmental problems, their cross-border effects and the need for concerted collective international action. The United Nations' decision to hold the Stockholm conference was taken at the General Assembly. There was also a conference held at Founex, Switzerland, in 1971 whose report informed the agenda for the Stockholm conference.

Since the 1970s, there were a number of environmental disasters across the world that not only attracted attention, but also influenced the discussion on environmental issues. These events informed policy-making at national levels in a big way. In 1979, at Three Mile Island in Pennsylvania, a nuclear accident occurred, which led to around 2.5 million curies of radiation being released. Several elderly people died, and it was reported that there were cancers detected in cattle and more than the usual number of premature births and birth defects among humans in the area. A tightening of safety procedures around nuclear reactor installations globally was an outcome of the disaster. Despite all these measures, there was a nuclear meltdown at Chernobyl in Russia in 1986, which was a thousand times worse than the Three Mile incident, resulting in the deaths of thousands of innocent people.

An event that brought into focus the actions of multinational companies in the developing world was the Bhopal Gas Tragedy of 1984, where a cyanide gas spill in a chemical plant operated by Union Carbide resulted in over 20,000 deaths. Over a 100,000 people still suffer from the aftermath of the chemical spill. Another landmark environmental disaster was the Exxon Valdez oil spill in 1989, when an oil tanker collided with a reef in the ocean. It led to the death of over 200,000 sea birds, 250 bald eagles (a protected species), thousands of sea otters, and even many killer whales. A more persistent problem was discovered in 1985 with respect to the *ozone hole* on top of the Antarctic Circle. The lower concentration of a protective layer of ozone in the earth's stratosphere would lead to the infiltration of harmful ultraviolet radiation that was posing a problem for human health. As the number of near-misses and disasters in every corner of the world kept growing, coupled with increasing publicity and awareness, pressures to prevent such events increased on businesses, governments, and multilateral institutions.

With the help of a quick review of major international efforts at sustainable development, we will focus on a few core challenges faced by the international community—the institutions and instruments available for action. International action requires cooperation and consensus building at two distinct levels. First, there is the need to agree on a common solution, which requires shared action by nation states such as reduction in emission of greenhouse gases. Secondly, there are many problems that require local action within the nation state, such as conserving groundwater or biodiversity within a country's borders. These actions are usually decided autonomously by the nation state and implemented within its own borders. Such actions need to be consistent across nations, which imply that countries must have a shared vision about sustainability and arrive at very similar sets of priorities for action. In this sense, the shared vision has to emerge from a spirit of cooperation.

Efforts at Cooperative Solutions: International Milestones

The first major international meeting that took place was at Stockholm where the United Nations Conference on Human Environment was held in 1972. This was the first global recognition of the link between human behavior and environmental problems. It was widely acknowledged that the problems faced by developing countries are different from those faced by the developed world. Yet, there was a need to reach a consensus to address the imminent environmental crisis. It was also as an outcome of the conference that a new focus of public discourse was established, namely, that there need not always be a harsh tradeoff between environmental conservation and material economic development. It led to the creation of the United Nations Environment Program (UNEP), and the concept of sustainable development was discussed as a possible solution in reconciling environment and development. 1972 also saw the release of the Club of Rome report called the Limits to Growth. This report highlighted the fact that business-as-usual along with prevalent consumption patterns of society, if left unchanged, would inevitably lead to a shortage of natural resources and irreversible degradation of the natural environment.

The next big milestone was the Earth Summit held at Rio in 1992, but during the intervening decades, there were a number of interesting developments that took place. The Global 2000 project and report, commissioned by President Carter of the United States in 1977, and released in 1980, was the first attempt by a nation to prepare a 20-year outlook on probable changes in the world's population, resources, economy, and environment, using the best available data and computer models of the time. In 1983, the World Commission on Environment and Development was formed with Gro Harlem Brundtland as the chairperson. The mandate of this commission was to propose within three years the following solutions. First was the identification of long-term environmental strategies that would help achieve sustainable development in the next (21st) century. Second, the commission was supposed to suggest ways and means of achieving greater cooperation between countries at different stages of economic and social development. The binding factor would be the shared concern for the environment. Third, it was supposed to help the international community deal more effectively with nature. Lastly, it was supposed to define shared perceptions of long-term solutions. This commission's definition of sustainable development is still the most commonly used one. There were a number of other systematic reports and conferences that took place in the 1980s as a precursor to the Earth Summit in Rio. Worldwatch Institute, an American think-tank first published a comprehensive State of the World Report in 1984. In 1987, Our Common Future was published, which focused on the need for economic growth that was environmentally and socially sustainable. It also identified the three pillars of sustainable development, namely, the environment, the economy, and society. It stimulated a new discourse on sustainable development, looking for public policy guidelines.

In 1986, the International Union for Conservation of Nature (IUCN) held a conference on Environment and Development. The IUCN, formed in 1948, is an influential organization comprising government and civil society organizations (CSOs). It is among the most diverse environmental networks and has emerged as a global authority on the status of the natural world, with expertise in species survival, environmental law, protected areas, social and economic policy, ecosystem management and education, and communication. Combining the latest science with the traditional knowledge of local communities, IUCN meetings have produced several key international environmental agreements including the Convention on Biological Diversity (CBD), the Convention on International Trade in Endangered Species (CITES), the World Heritage Convention, and the Ramsar Convention on Wetlands.

An expert level conference was held in 1985 in Villach, Austria, where scientific data and evidence was presented that indicated the possibility of climate change and global warming. This was the precursor of the Intergovernmental Panel on Climate Change (IPCC) that was set up in 1988. The IPCC has evolved into an influential forum for analyzing the scientific evidence available and also making suggestions for adapting to and mitigating climate change through appropriate policies. It is currently in the 6th cycle of assessing the most recently available data on climate change and related matters. In 1982, the UN Convention on the Law of the Sea was adopted after nine years of negotiation. This was the first set of material rules defining and enforcing environmental standards. Problems of the open seas as a global commons had not been addressed before.

The dangers pertaining to the ozone hole led to the Montreal Protocol being adopted in 1987 to reduce the use of substances that resulted in the depletion of the ozone layer. Considered to be the most successful environmental treaty till date, the Montreal Protocol was adopted by 196 nation states and the European Union, and the positive effects of reducing the manufacture and use of ozone-depleting substances is evident in the gradual reparation of the depleted ozone layer.

In 1992, the United Nations Conference on Environment and Development was held at Rio de Janeiro (often called the Earth Summit). 178 nations and over 2,000 CSOs were represented by over 17,000 participants at this gathering. The major outcomes of the Earth Summit were the Rio Declaration on Environment and Development, Agenda 21, CBD, Forest Principles, UN Framework Convention on Climate Change (UNFCCC), and the Commission on Sustainable Development (CSD). The Rio declaration comprised 27 principles intended to guide (non-binding) sustainable development policies around the world. Some of the key highlights of this declaration were that humans would be at the center of all policies, states should facilitate increased public participation, internalize environmental costs by using economic instruments, environmental impact assessments should be undertaken for new projects, and environmental issues should be integrated into development planning.

Agenda 21 was a blueprint for global action aligned with national and local action plans with the task of balancing environmental economic and social objectives. Four broad sections for action are social and economic dimensions; conservation and management of resources for development; strengthening the role of major groups, such as youth, women, NGOs; and the means of implementation, which includes science education and technology transfers. Once again, Agenda 21 is non-binding. In comparison, the UNFCCC, signed initially by 153 nations, to reduce emissions of greenhouse gases (GHGs) has been ratified by enough nations to be implemented as binding. Similarly, the CBD is a binding agreement signed by 156 nations dealing with the exploitation of genetic material and biodiversity conservation. The CSD was established to monitor Agenda 21. However, it neither has the power to make binding resolutions nor has resources to finance programs under the Agenda.

In 1994, the Global Environment Facility (GEF), set up in 1991, was restructured to ensure that international aid could be used more by developing countries to achieve the objectives of the Rio summit. This was followed by the World Summit for Social Development at Copenhagen in 1995, where, for the first time, the international community expressed a clear commitment to eradicate absolute poverty. Extending the UNFCCC, the Kyoto Protocol was signed by 192 countries in 1997 to implement the objectives of reducing GHG concentrations so as to stem global warming. Based on the principle of common but differentiated responsibility, the protocol puts a higher obligation on countries from the developed world to reduce their current emissions than the developing world. In line with the Rio summit, several economic instruments to facilitate GHG reductions were introduced.

As a follow-up to the Copenhagen summit, the UN millennium summit was held in 2000 in Geneva where the Millennium Development Goals (MDGs) were declared. There were eight MDGs agreed to by all the worlds' countries and all leading development institutions. The goals to be achieved within 15 years were: eradication of extreme poverty and hunger, achievement of universal primary education, gender equality and empowerment of women, reduction of child mortality and improvement of maternal health, combating HIV AIDS and malaria, ensuring environmental sustainability, and developing a global partnership for sustainability.

The next major global event was the World Summit on Sustainable Development held in Johannesburg in 2002. This summit is often referred to as Rio + 10. This summit established the need to assess progress and implementation of Agenda 21, though these were non-binding. The UN also affirmed its commitment to facilitate the implementations of MDGs. No new conventions emerged out of the meeting. The focus was on the social aspects of sustainability, namely, fighting poverty and debt while increasing access to resources and international development aid.

As the terminal date of the Kyoto Protocol was 2012, the 15th session of the Conference of Parties in the UNFCCC was held at Copenhagen in December 2009 to address the concern. A new political accord emerged out of this meeting where all the major economies of the world made explicit pledges regarding reduction of GHG emissions. This was the first time China participated. This accord was preceded by lot of bitter debates and divisions among the participating countries. The United States aimed to have a legally binding instrument agreed upon by all the countries, but failed in its efforts. The salient features of the accord included a goal for limiting global temperature increase to 2°C and broad terms for reporting and verifying each country's pledged action. There was also a commitment made by the developed countries collectively to provide 30 billion dollars to help the developing countries reduce emissions, conserve nature, and adapt to climate change during the period 2010 to 2012. This was supposed to go up to 100 billion dollars a year by 2020. This accord, however, failed to bring about a clear roadmap for a treaty that would have binding commitments by nations.

The Paris Agreement, reached in December 2015, which came into force in November 2016, is a break from the past in climate change negotiations because, for the first time, it got all countries to make pledges for reduction of GHGs (Intended Nationally Determined Contributions—INDCs) to contain the effects of climate change to keep temperatures from rising by less than 2°C. Additionally, the Paris Agreement aims to increase appropriate financial flows for the purpose, promote new technologies, and enhance capacities to deal with the national objectives of each country. Each nation would determine its own contributions and report regularly on their emissions and status of their implementation efforts. A review would be taken in 2018, and global stocktaking would take place subsequently every five years. So far, 55 parties to the convention, accounting for about 55 percent of global GHG emissions have deposited their instruments of ratification, acceptance, approval, or accession with the depository.

In October 2016, 170 countries successfully negotiated a legally binding agreement to cut down 90 percent of HFCs (hydrofluorocarbons) and, as a result, take out 0.5°C out of future global warming. The aim is to reduce HFCs is a phased manner beginning in 2019 for the developed world. About a 100 developing countries would start taking action from 2024 and India, Pakistan, and some Gulf states would do so by 2028 on the grounds that these nations need to grow economically. HFCs are used in air-conditioning systems, particularly in the developing countries in the world, but because China and India adopted air-conditioning in homes, offices, and cars, the growth of HFCs became alarming as they are supposed to be far more destructive than CO_2 in their impact on climate. Only a handful of chemical companies produce HFCs, making it easier for governments' to put pressure on a single industry. Alternatives in the form of hydrocarbons, nitrogen, and ammonia are widely available, approved and considered safe for air-conditioning and refrigeration.

All the major developments discussed were, in a way, outcomes of three major meetings that took place since the 1970s; the 1972 Stockholm Convention, which focused on the environmental issues; the 1992 Rio Convention that focused on the economic aspects of managing environmental problems; and 2002 Johannesburg Convention, which focused on the social dimensions of development in harmony with nature. The three conventions, together with their distinct emphases, can be viewed as having contributed to the three pillars of sustainable development where current economic development and future development can be consistently attained without irreversibly damaging nature. We now turn our discussion to how the structures of governance for sustainable development have emerged over the past three or four decades.

Structures of Governance

The ways in which the world has reacted to the need for environmental protection and sustainable development has witnessed new players, decision-makers, and collaborative partnerships across countries, business firms, and CSOs.[1] New instruments have also emerged where there is less emphasis on control and more to do with incentives, as well as ethical convictions to promote the desired changes. There are seemingly unconnected events across the world. For instance, New York City has paid landowners in upstate New York to improve water quality for the city. The

---

[1] This section draws from Agrawal and Lemos (2007).

World Wildlife Fund is working with Chevron in Papua New Guinea to conserve biodiversity. Similarly, the voluntary nature of corporate social responsibility has helped attract new ways of working out problems facing the environment. These unconnected events are actually linked by the common fact that all address environmental problems.

Till a few decades ago, environmental governance had remained in the exclusive purview of a nation state. One of the reasons why a broad variety of actors can help bring about novel solutions to environmental problems is because of the sheer complexity, ubiquity, and urgency of the environmental problems faced by humanity that have economic and social consequences. Hence, collaborative solutions are likely to be much more efficient than depending on policymakers of a nation state alone. These new forms of governance involving more nuanced analysis of problems are referred to as hybrid forms of governance where markets, states, and communities all play equally important roles. The relationship between state and the market is reflected in the increasing numbers of public–private partnerships. Where the state and the community collaborate for management of natural resources, the governance structures that emerge are referred to as co-management. Public social partnerships are the relationships that markets and communities enter into, for instance, in ventures such as eco-tourism.

A striking feature of the emerging forms of sustainability governance is the increasing role of market actors and market-based instruments. Even communities try to resolve their problems by taking recourse to some form of market-based solutions. Some of the solutions could be based on a proxy valuation of nature, for example. It should be noted, however, that governance should not swing from an over dependence on the state (as in the past) to an over dependence on markets. It should be kept in mind that markets perform well only when the state provides adequate information, well-defined property rights, facilitates competition, identifies and addresses market externalities, and helps reduce transaction costs. A greater reliance on markets must also go hand-in-hand with safeguarding of stakeholders' interests and values and protecting endangered ecosystems and threatened species.

Hybrid forms of governance are not always perfect. There are many experiments taking place. New concerns and issues are coming to the fore, such as whether such forms of governance commodify nature as an unbridled market system is wont to do. Another concern with hybrid governance is that it promotes more efficient use of natural resources, leading to faster extraction and possible technological alternatives being found. This exclusive focus on a purely anthropogenic view of nature could be to the detriment of other species and even future generations.

What, then, would be the best way forward in addressing issues of governance in a complex world, especially the problems associated with the distribution of costs and benefits? Germane to all environmental problems is the need for local action, which is also consistent with some bigger global vision of shared goals. It is in this sense that we might see in the near future an erosion of the nation state's power to control with a greater role of governing the environment at the grassroots level. We are also likely to see a greater international role in bringing the world together to create a shared action plan.

Challenges of Global Governance

One of the biggest difficulties of attaining effective global governance for sustainable development is the problem of collective action. We had seen some of the reasons for this when we discussed this in Chapter 3. However, it is not true that all attempts at attaining global solutions have failed. For instance, the Montreal Protocol was a success because of a number of specific factors. It dealt with a very specific issue, and there was an effective leadership in negotiating the concept of common but differentiated responsibility. Though the science required was not completely definitive, the precautionary principle ensured that negotiating parties refrained from taking unnecessary risk. The chemical and allied sectors, such as refrigeration, were willing and ready to innovate, and this helped the governments prioritize facilitation of long-term research. Funding was also made available, and the Montreal Protocol provided a stable framework that allowed the relevant industries to plan for the future. Technological innovation and possibilities were assessed by an independent technology panel, which was successful in identifying potential innovations. A final reason for the success of the Montreal Protocol was the compliance procedure. While this was designed as a non-punitive procedure, it monitored wayward and laggard countries and helped them back into compliance.

The results of its success were also clearly evident over time with respect to the size of the ozone hole.

Other attempts at global governance, such as the Kyoto Protocol, have been marked by much greater degrees of complexity and differences in short-term interests of the developed and developing economies. Hence, collective action has been much more difficult. Because of this difficulty, attempts at global environmental governance have seen the proliferation of multilateral environmental agreements and the fragmentation of governance between state and non-state actors, including a large body of CSOs. This has often led to a lack of cooperation and coordination among these organizations and duplication of effort, leading to an inefficient use of financial, and as well as human resources. Little wonder that, in such a situation, global environmental governance has been marked by a lack of enforcement, compliance, and implementation. The recent past has also witnessed global environmental governance being pursued by organizations that are not specialized in such matters. For instance, the WTO, World Bank, and the UNDP while trying to promote rule-based trade and facilitate economic development have often had their impact on environmental aspects of trade and development. On some matters, there has been a lack of consistency between the approach of these institutions and other specialized government agencies.

A key issue that emerges from these challenges to governance is the fact that some nations and organizations focus more on the *sustainable* in sustainable development, while other focus on the *development* aspect of sustainable development. These two approaches, if designed separately, will not necessarily lead to sustainable development as being equivalent to a non-decreasing productive capital base for the whole world. To get these two together and make environmental governance coherent for sustainable development, we need greater knowledge that is shared and accepted, as well as political will from policymakers and negotiators, which would provide the necessary global leadership.

The Way Forward: Alternate Models of Global Governance

Policymakers and academics involved in environmental issues have been debating on ways and means of improving global environmental governance, with the key challenge of how to design an institutional framework that would best protect the global environment.[2] A few alternative conceptual models are often put forward in the debate. One approach, referred to as the compliance model, identifies non-compliance as the critical constraint in effective governance. Hence, proponents advocate the creation of a body of institutions that would include whole nation states, as well as private actors, accountable for creating environmental damage and not complying with international agreements. Some have even suggested the creation of a World Environment Court along the lines of the European Court of Human Rights.

A second approach refers to creating a completely new organization even outside the United Nations with full responsibilities on all environmental matters, both in terms of forming rules and regulations and to ensure compliance. Proposals have suggested the creation of a Global Environmental Organization along the lines of the WTO. This would provide an opportunity to put together the best features of all organizations involved in global environmental governance within one setup.

A third approach suggests strengthening of existing United Nations organizations, rather than creating a super-organization beyond it. The suggestion has been to strengthen the UNEP into a specialized agency and give it more financial muscle and regulatory authority. A suggestion has been made to upgrade UNEP into an UNEO (UN Environmental Organization). An advantage of this would be that the organization could draw upon the large experience and knowledge of the various arms of the United Nations.

A fourth proposition is an organizational streamlining of existing agencies without necessarily merging them into a single body. Better coordination could come, for instance, through forming clusters of organizations, which could be specialized in certain areas of functioning, which could either be regional in scope of issue based. The logic would be to keep the advantages of smaller organization and their efficiency by ensuring coherence between them.

Finally, there is a model referred to as the multiple-actors model, which supports the multiplicity of actors and interactions between them.

---

[2] This section draws from Najam et. al (2006).

In this case, the exchange of ideas and learning and the ability to create innovative solutions would be the greatest synergy that would emerge. Advocates of this position argue that governance is easier for specific environmental issues. The real need for global governance is to integrate all these and transcend into the large context of sustainable development, which is more complex and harder to quantify. They suggest having a General Agreement on Environment and Development to codify universally accepted sustainability principles to guide future multilateral environmental agreements while retaining multiple channels of implementation.

While there is no consensus on which model to use and how it would actually emerge, there are some positive signals that are discernible. First, there is an emerging consensus between policymakers, businesses, academics, and CSOs that some reform is necessary and inevitable. If this does not happen, then environmental governance would remain meaningless words. The second encouraging sign has been that the number of organizations, as well as the nature of organizations calling for reform, has changed. These include international platforms, national governments, international NGOs, and many other local bodies as well as local communities. Finally, the cumulative experience of many attempts at environmental governance has given the advocates for reform a far-clearer understanding of what might work and what might not and what kinds of mechanisms would be politically feasible, as well as conceptually desirable.

Whatever be the form of global governance that might emerge, all action plans are based on perceptions of our relationships with nature, other forms of life, and future generations. These perceptions are intricately related to our moral judgments about these relationships. The moral judgments can be of different kinds. The following chapter analyses ethics in the context of sustainability.

CHAPTER 11

Ethics and Sustainable Development

Sustainable development requires human beings to make environmentally and socially responsible decisions to protect the species and the earth. These decisions are made by individuals, a community, institutions, or nations. The decisions involve views and perceptions about the planet's ecological and social environment and the impact of human activities on it. The judgments based on these perceptions are essentially ethical in nature. Here, personal beliefs, social experiences, and awareness of human–nature interactions play a critical part in the formation of ethical views. Sustainability is not merely a goal to be attained, but also a value based outlook about life on the planet.

We start our discussion by looking at alternative ethical positions on the human–nature relationship. This is followed by a discussion on approaches to attain distributive justice, which is a necessary condition for sustainability. From trying to understand ethics from an individual perspective, we then look at a particular instance of formation of a collective ethic in the context of a firm. Challenges in developing a collective ethic and social norms are discussed last.

The Human–Nature Relationship

How human beings perceive the problem of sustainable development depends to a large extent on how their relationship with nature is comprehended. There could be a multiplicity of perceptions, which would lead to alternative moral positions that could be adopted (Newman 2011). A common view of the world would be where human beings are essential and the rest of nature is perceived from this central position. This view is referred to as an anthropocentric one. An alternative view, perhaps not as prominent as the first one, looks at human beings as part of nature at par with other species. This view is referred to as a biocentric one. These two views could be sub-divided into consequentialist and deontological ethics. Sustainable development is a goal that could be attained through different paths depending on alternative ethical decisions taken at the individual or policy level. The consequentialist position focuses more on the goodness of outcomes, given a broad objective to be attained. The deontologist position, on the other hand, focuses more on the nature of the means to the end to be attained. To them, a good consequence may not be acceptable if the means adopted to attain it is not right. Hence, a variety of ethical positions are possible in the context of the human–nature relationship. These are briefly discussed as follows.

Anthropocentric ethics posit that nature is of instrumental value and is there to be used for the benefit of human beings. This ethical position is consequentialist. If, for instance, one could extract resources for human consumption, then it would be a positive consequence. On the other hand, any natural calamity that has an adverse effect on society would be termed as a negative consequence, and outcomes would be viewed exclusively in terms of the impact on human wellbeing. Most mainstream approaches to the understanding of economic development and change view nature through this ethical lens.

In some cases, the anthropocentric view might attribute an intrinsic value to nature, and hence would consider it to be part of human duty to conserve nature. Any activity that despoils or degrades nature would be considered morally wrong, even if it improves human wellbeing in the short term. This approach is deontological, in the sense that the consequence of conservation of nature is not of any special importance.

In the biocentric approach, human beings are considered as essential as all other life forms in nature. A biocentric and consequentialist ethical position would posit that nature is of instrumental value for the requirements of life for all living beings. Hence, any change in the environment would have to be evaluated in terms of its impact on all species. For instance, an environmental impact that negatively affects a particular species, say owls, but creates new opportunities for human beings would not be acceptable unless it could be demonstrated that there is a net gain in the movement toward sustainability.

Finally, a biocentric deontological ethical position would imply that nature has an intrinsic value for all living beings and should be preserved, independent of what nature's effect is on particular living beings. For instance, if in a storm, a bird's nest is destroyed, the deontological view maintains that nothing can be done about the situation because both the storm and birds nest are part of nature, and this is a natural phenomenon.

Both anthropocentrism and biocentrism can be problematic in practical situations. In an anthropocentric perspective, it might be asked whether our obligation, or the value we ascribe to human beings, is more important than that ascribed to other living beings. For instance, one could argue that does anthropocentricism imply a situation where other living beings have no rights at all or some rights that are subordinate to the rights of humans. Would it be morally acceptable if we kill animals for food? Biocentrism, on the other hand, implies that all living beings are considered to be equally important in the natural order of things. However, it is well accepted in philosophy that all living beings do not possess moral agency, in the sense that they are conscious of their actions and can explain those actions in terms of why they were enacted.

Another problem stems from the importance of putting a value to different kinds of outcomes that affect nature. In justifying human actions to protect and preserve the environment, some estimate of the value of protecting nature or the cost of despoiling nature has to be made. This is not easily done as already discussed in Chapter 6. In many cases, as the risks are not known with any certainty, risk aversion may be the best strategy to adopt. This is the notion of the precautionary principle, which states that the avoidance of loss is preferred to compensation after damage, when the extent of damage expected is not known beforehand. An alternative decision could be taken on the basis that because the risks are unknown, especially in the context of their magnitude and incidence, it would be best to ignore it. For instance, policies pertaining to the promotion of genetically modified organisms differ among countries depending on which stance they adopt.

Most ethical positions adopted in the literature on sustainable development take an anthropocentric view, but often incorporate nuanced positions which have biocentric implications. In other words, there is a value to biodiversity that is imputed only because in the ultimate analysis the preservation of biodiversity is essential to human survival.

Ethics and Distributive Justice

In this section, we will discuss the essential characteristic of sustainable development where issues of ethics and distributive justice come in. Sustainable development deals with both the present and the future (both short- and long-term future) in a basic yet incomplete way. Some action has to be taken to make development sustainable so that future generations of human beings can continue to live by meeting their material needs. If no action is taken at the present time, then there could be (non-zero probability) a shortage of resources in the future. This, in turn, could lead to catastrophic costly change.

Let us first consider the present generation of human beings inhabiting the earth. We have rich countries and poor countries as well as rich and poor people within each country. If we view the major environmental issues that could lead to unsustainability, then the rich countries have played a major role in the creation of those problems, such as greenhouse gases, ocean acidification, loss of biodiversity, rising toxic pollution, and the ozone hole. The poorer countries, on the other hand, have made a much smaller contribution in this regard. If large environmental problems crop up, then it is more likely that the poor countries and the poor people of the world will be most adversely affected. For instance, the overwhelming majority of poor people live in the tropical regions of the world, and the hot and arid regions are supposed to be affected the most through declining agricultural productivity. This loss of productivity could come from shortage of water, higher temperatures, and the loss of nutrients in the top soil. Food shortages would lead to higher prices, which, in turn, would cause economic hardship. This is an issue of distributive justice for the present generation. Had there been less disparity, the ability of the poor to adapt to adverse situations would be better.

If we consider the future generations, the question of distributive justice arises when our actions in the present damage the environment to such an extent that future generations are unable to live and enjoy a material standard of living that the present generation has experienced. This could only be corrected if the present generation made some changes in their lifestyles and ways of producing goods and services, so as to ensure that in the future people do not get hurt by becoming poorer. This intergenerational distributive justice gets intrinsically connected with the issue of intragenerational distributive justice. The practical issue in this matter boils down to who pays for ensuring sustainable development. It would be unjust to expect the poor countries or the poor people of the world to pay for correcting problems that they had little role in creating and are more likely to get hurt in the event of environmental disaster.

Utilitarianism

We now take a look at few important ethical positions that have been used by economists in their evaluation of distributive justice. The philosophy of utilitarianism goes back to Bentham (1907) where the subjective understanding was that economic activities were undertaken to provide satisfaction or utility (also see Mill, Bentham, and Ryan 1987). The state of affairs of a society or an individual was judged by the total utility of that state. Society would be considered to be better off if total utility increased. This total utility would be made by aggregation of the utility of each individual. If one judged a social state in terms of its total utility alone, then two important things would be missing in that calculation. The first would be that, if individuals looked at the natural environment purely from an instrumental point of view, then issues of environmental damage would not be addressed at all because utility would be dependent on the individuals' consumption or income, which could be enhanced by a greater use of exhaustible natural resources. The calculus of individual utility could lead to improvements in utility only to the extent that it increased the measure through consumption or income. The second implication of this would be that a high level of utility for a society could be consistent with a great deal of inequality in consumption and incomes. Hence, the utilitarian ethic is oblivious to environmental damage, as well as a great deal of social and economic inequity.

There have been critiques of ethics of utilitarianism (Sen 1987, Sen and Williams (ed) 1982) in the way it has been used in economic theory.

Epistemic foundations of utilitarian welfare economics were seen as incurably defective

—(Sen 2002, p. 71)

One way of reconciling environment to the utilitarian calculus could be to assume that each individual assigns a distinct value to environmental quality over and above his or her consumption or income. Hence, utility would be defined over environmental quality and individual consumption or income. In such a situation, a rise in income concomitant with a dramatic fall in environmental quality would not necessarily lead to a rise in total utility. As far as inequalities are concerned, it is easy to see that, for a given amount of income, redistribution from the rich to the poor would necessarily increase total utility. The reason is that it is generally considered that incremental utility from additional income diminishes. Hence, taking one unit of income from the rich would reduce total utility by a smaller amount than the increase in utility when that unit was transferred to a poor person. Hence, utilitarianism may not be inconsistent with having a more even distribution of income, though mechanically summing up individual utilities could hide this important characteristic.

We had argued that inequality was ethically unjustifiable in the context of distributive justice. However, modern economies in the recent past have been judging economic performance to a large extent by the growth rate of GDP alone. This has resulted in sharply increasing inequalities, which many economists have commented on (Stiglitz 2012, Piketty 2014, 2015). The persistence of inequality make it difficult to use utilitarian calculus to move toward sustainable development.

Nozick and the Importance of Non-Coercion

Another philosopher whose ideas have had a significant influence in the ethical justification of a market economic system was Robert Nozick (1974). Nozick argued that the means to an end were as important as the end itself. Thus, if the end is to reduce the extent of carbon accumulation to minimize the impact of climate change, the means to do so must not be coercive like the state using command and control policies. If the right to life is the most important right a human being possesses, then the right not to be coerced gets precedence over all other rights because without this guarantee life itself would be jeopardized.

In the context of the political economy, this position has a number of implications. One implication is that any economic outcome that was the result of voluntary (non-coercive) transactions would be deemed to be fair and just, provided two conditions were satisfied. First, the transaction of exchange took place where the things exchanged were obtained through previous non coercive actions. The second condition would be that all individuals are deemed to be self-owners, in the sense that they not only own their own bodies, mind, and labor, but also own things (material goods) as private property. Another implication is that natural objects freely available in the environment, for instance, trees, land, and water bodies, can be acquired as private property. In this philosophical position, nature becomes a *thing* to be acquired and used for human benefits. There is no concern with respect to coercion of nature. Yet another implication is that, if the outcome of a set of market transactions is deemed to be fair and just, then any attempt to redistribute resources and goods would be deemed as coercion of some people who would have to give up their entitlements. Hence, any taxation by any authority would be considered as an act of coercion. It may be noted that Nozick was not in favor of a stateless anarchy, but in favor of an ultra-minimal state, which could raise taxes as a special case to provide essential services: a service (police, army) to protect private property and a retributive justice system to punish those who coerce others.

Rawls and the Provision of Basic Goods

John Rawls' theory of justice (1971) is another philosophical position, which has been extensively used in the economics literature to understand the fairness or otherwise of a state of affairs. Rawls argument is that market economies are quite efficient in terms of allocation of resources among alternative uses and the production of goods and services. However, the distributional outcome of this could well be terribly unequal and this would be unjustifiable. Unlike Nozick, Rawls argues for an interventionist state, which would redistribute resources according to a particular criterion.

Rawls' theory is premised on two basic principles, the principle of maximin and the difference principle. The maximin principle emerges from an abstract situation referred to as the original position where economic agents who will comprise a society are handicapped by a *veil of ignorance*. Each agent knows that, in playing the market game, some will end up rich and others will end up poor. The ignorance is about not knowing who will end up becoming rich or poor. Hence, Rawls argued that it is in everyone's interest to agree that the worst-off individual is made as well-off as possible through an effective redistributive mechanism, which does not go so far as to take away resources from the rich in a way that reverses the ranking. This is maximizing the position of the minimally placed individual. Here, Rawls made an elaborate case for the provision of a set of basic goods for this purpose. His understanding of basic goods was quite broad. Liberty and freedom were included as basic goods and services. The second principle, referred to as the difference principle, argues that inequalities in wealth and power are justified only to the extent that they reside in positions that are accessible to all, and this inequality is necessary to ensure the effective implementation of the maximin principle. For instance, the head of a democratic state is more powerful than other citizens, but the position is open to all citizens. It is also evident that a representative government is required to undertake the redistribution to achieve a socially optimal outcome.

In the context of sustainable development, the Rawlsian position is important because it leads to more equal distributions of income and wealth. The position can be further augmented by including environmental goods along with liberty, freedom, and other goods and services as a part of the basket of basic goods. If this is not done, then there could be outcomes that are contradictory in nature. Environmental pollution for instance, or damaging nature in any way would be justified if it enhanced the incomes of the poorest people or in an international situation of the poorest countries through a redistributive mechanism.

Sen and Capabilities

Amartya Sen has been another economist-philosopher whose work has significantly influenced economic thinking (1985, 2001). Sen's framework builds on rights and liberties as something that gives an individual entitlement to a *thing* of value. From society's point of view, if there is a severe deprivation of entitlements, then the outcome is likely to be more unequal. Sen would consider such a distributive outcome as unjust. To address this inequality, Sen argues about the importance on individual human capabilities, such as enjoying good health or being educated. As human beings, each of us tries to achieve a chosen set of capabilities. This choice is not only dependent on one's preferences, but is also conditioned to a very large extent by the social deal available to each.

A simple example will suffice. Consider a poor person having the right to get food from the state. This would give the individual an entitlement to receive a specified quantity of subsidized food from the public distribution system. The capability obtained from consuming this food would be adequate nutrition and become part of a bigger freedom to enjoy good health. The social situation faced might be such that the person has limited access to education or health care facilities. The nutrition level attained in the long haul would be severely affected by the lack of medical attention. Similarly, the lack of education could well restrict even a person of good health and adequate nutrition to function in terms of many activities where good health and basic education complement one another to provide a set of fundamentally important capabilities.

The ultimate goal of an expanding sphere of capabilities, in Sen's framework, is not merely about material goods and services. The goals include achieving freedom from hunger, ill health, insecurity, and homelessness, as well as self-actualization, recognition from the community, and having fulfilling relationships with other people.

This framework has important implications as far as the human–nature relationship is concerned. Take for instance the human capability of enjoying good health. This could be hampered if there is unchecked pollution in air and water or a sudden decline in agricultural productivity. A clean environment is essential for achieving many basic capabilities. Similarly, a loss of biodiversity could seriously interrupt the food chain, leading to health-related problems for human beings. This framework is not only restricted to human beings, but can be extended to all living beings if a reasonably common capability that human beings wish to enjoy could be defined in terms of existing harmoniously in the world with other living beings. Sen (2004) also argues that living in harmony with all living beings may not be restricted to a narrow view of beings that currently inhabit the planet. Living a harmonious life would require a commitment to make sure that those who inherit the earth are not left on ruins generated by the current generation.

Extending Sen's position, one might prescribe environmental protection as a human right, which leads to the freedom to use and enjoy nature without despoiling it in any irreversible way. This, however, has some practical limitations because, to be effective, it has to be made into an international law. Apart from arriving at a global consensus on the details of such a law, there are legal complications of allowing proceedings on behalf of people who are yet unborn. (Finkmoore 2010)

Business Ethics

Businesses are an important set of institutions that determine the human–nature relationship and its impact on the planet. As they are responsible, both for driving consumption and for production activities, their role is crucial in bringing about sustainable practices and influencing social values. Ethics usually considers how an individual moral agent views a situation and arrives at a reason for action. It is essentially individualistic. When discussing business actions, a fundamental problem arises in ascribing an ethical position to a set of individuals who comprise the organization or the firm. Within the firm, different individuals who take decisions can well have different moral positions on a particular issue. How then is the firm's ethical position arrived at? Is it always determined through a consensus based on debate and discussion, or is it ultimately determined by the head of the organization? Finally, is it possible to treat the firm as a moral individual on whose action we can pass judgment about right and wrong? It is a problem of collective or social ethic, which is often determined by the culture or values that are well regarded and promoted by the organization. Very often, the process of arriving at the firm's ethical position is not available in the public domain. For instance, the debate that can take place in a committee meeting might be reflected in the minutes of the meeting, but would hardly be available for public consumption.

Despite this, much can be inferred from the actions of firms on various issues that bear upon the contribution made toward sustainable development. It is expected that all firms that come under the purview of different kinds of environmental regulations would comply with the requirements. This would be the minimal ethical responsibility of the firm. Many firms can be observed to go beyond the regulatory compliance and voluntarily adopt a new technology or new processes, products, or raw materials (see Chapter 8). Obviously, these firms make a greater contribution toward sustainable development. If firms adopt such actions, it is consistent with their business strategy to grow and sustain themselves. This is an outcome of the business environment that the firm operates in coupled with a self-enlightened leadership at the helm of the firm. Any business firm's relationship with its customers, vendors, and employees reflects the ethics and culture of the organization. For instance, in dealing with its internal processes or with purchases made from vendors, the firm may insist on certain sustainable practices that are environmentally friendly. The firm's relationship with its customers is more nuanced. Customers' tastes and preferences along with their price sensitivity of demand determine which goods and services are sold and at what prices. Would a firm agree to educate its customers into becoming more sustainable in their consumption? Would it be transparent about the long-term sustainability implications of production and consumption of different goods and services?

There could be an ethical dilemma if the firm finds itself in a situation where, by reducing a social cost they are creating, they will incur a large private cost internal to the firm. Alternatively, going beyond regulatory compliance and contributing to sustainable development may not align well with the firm's core business strategy. Should the firm relook and revamp its business strategy, or should it continue with business as usual, while being a *good* corporate citizen by complying? It may be noted that the corporate citizen in question is not an individual, but a set of individuals whose collective decision is observed. This makes it more complex than individual ethics. However, we do observe ethical decisions that are agreed upon by a collective. We also often witness similar patterns on ethical behavior in a community, which are often referred to as social norms. It is to these issues that we now turn.

Collective Ethic and Social Norms

We have discussed in earlier chapters that any policy that would facil-itate sustainable development would necessarily have to be a collective (national) decision and would reflect a particular ethical position regard-ing the changes that would be brought about. For example, the choice of a social discount rate would be determined by the social planner or policymaker, but it would be reflective of the choices of society. To arrive at a consensual social ethic requires constant engagement with society at large, where public debates and discussions should be used to inform the final social choice. This is more challenging than it sounds because of the plurality in individual ethics and power relationships among individuals and collectives.

Individual ethical positions can vary for a number of reasons, which lead to a heterogeneity of judgments of right and wrong, or good and bad. The first reason is that individuals are different and their own imbibed values from society and family could vary widely. The individual's eco-nomic position, educational attainment, life experiences all contribute to the making of a particular ethic that he or she possesses. The individual's ethical position might change over time too. The position adopted may also be quite contextual, where the individual's assessment of the conse-quences of a decision or action may change. An individual may have a moral position where telling lies is unethical. Nevertheless, in a specific situation, the individual may find it acceptable to lie when the conse-quence is directly beneficial to him or her.

Another reason why ethical norms might differ is due to cultural differences. More often than not, culture-specific ethics often play an important role in forming our opinion of social change. While it is true that there could be a lot of common norms across cultures, such as those regarding telling lies or physically hurting people, there are also a lot of differences across cultures, particularly when it comes to issues of indi-vidual advantage versus benefits accruing to a larger group. For instance, in many Asian cultures, the family, community, and the larger groups are given due importance in the ethics of redistributing resources. Western cultures are supposedly more individualistic, and hence, the individual's gain or loss is given a much larger weight than the concern for others.

While these statements may be quite general and there are bound to be variations from this stylized version, it is important to note that there is some basis for such generalizations. Over generations, a gradual collective ethic regarding social behavior emerges in every society, which gets transformed into a social norm guiding actual practice and influencing individual ethics.

Finally, there could be noticeable differences in the ethical stance adopted by different generations of people even within the same culture. One reason for this is that the younger generation often grows up in a substantially different social environment compared to its elders. The younger generation also learns to critique the senior generation in terms of what they did right or wrong for society at large. To take an example, in many countries, the current generation accepts priced bottled water as being a fair outcome in the context of failure of public supply of adequate and safe drinking water. Yet, a few decades ago, this would have been considered to be unethical, as it was amounting to gaining private benefit from a freely available public good.

The social consensus on the ethics of trying to attain sustainable development is not easy to arrive at. Education, sensitization about the importance of nature, trying to understand other peoples' positions, and tolerating some differences all contribute to the building of a consensus. In this context, the beginning of a social debate should focus around the crucial importance of caring about and sharing with other people. It should also harp on the importance of doing good wherever possible and refraining from doing harm.

We have discussed the difficulties in arriving at a collective ethic. It can be enormously challenging even within a small family to resolve ethical differences confronting the group. These difficulties become more and more challenging when we look at larger groups like a community or a society or a nation, as the extent of heterogeneity within these groups increase. In larger groups, what is often done to facilitate collective action is to empower a group, or even an individual (a parliament or a president of a nation), to take decisions on behalf of the larger group. When it comes to transnational collective action, the difficulties become well-nigh insurmountable.

CHAPTER 12

Toward Sustainable Development: Reform or Radical Change?

In Chapter 10, we had discussed the need for new institutions of governance, particularly at the global level. This is because the problem of sustainable development is a planetary one, and the natural environment is a global commons. We have also discussed the need for appropriate policies and interventions at the level of the nation or local communities, which should be consistent with a globally shared vision of sustainability. The role of local institutions would be to implement specific interventions based on the broad directives as developed by global institutions, which would play a critical role in shaping policy, as well as influencing people's thoughts and opinions on what constitutes an improvement in their quality of life. Thus, over and above issues of governance, there is the problem of changing the mode of *business as usual* into models that are more eco-efficient and socially sustainable. Consumers also need to change their preferences emerging from a better understanding of the urgency for protecting the environment for future generations.

This solution appears to be fairly straightforward when expressed on paper, but is hugely complex if it were to be implemented in real life. As discussed in previous chapters, there are underlying disparities in development goals at the local level as compared with the national or global levels, many of which are related to sustainability objectives. Similarly, the disparity in needs of the rich and poor, locally, and rich and poor countries, internationally, can result in deep mistrust among parties, which renders reaching a consensus near impossible. Individuals would have to change their mind-sets, the objectives of doing business may have to be recast, and all these have to be based on some international consensus on managing the environment. These changes, moreover, could take considerable time. On the other hand, moving toward sustainable development has acquired an urgency, given the evidence being generated about environmental degradation, climate change, and the possible imminent environmental disasters. If these changes are to come about and be effective in a relatively short period of time, the critical question would be as to whether market capitalism as we know it today could be adequately reformed.

In this context, there are many alternative beliefs and viewpoints. In what follows, we discuss two more prominent schools of thought. The first talks about the possibility of capitalism changing dramatically to become more nature-friendly (See Box 12.1), that is, resource allocation decisions would take into account the negative environmental externalities caused by them. The second is not as optimistic about drastic changes

Box 12.1 *Principles of natural capitalism*

Natural capitalism refers to a system where economic activity takes place in harmony with ecological principles, which accounts for the value of resources and services provided by nature. There are four interlinking principles that entail a different way for business to add value, innovate, and serve society by meeting its needs to the extent possible taking into account the true scarcity value of natural resources and ecosystem services.

The first principle revolves around radically increasing resource productivity by reducing the material and energy intensity of production processes, and redesigning the product if required. For example, using aluminum and other composite materials for vehicle bodies could increase their fuel efficiency by leaps and bounds. The second principle, often called biomimicry, relates to redesigning industry in line with how ecology works, without generating wastes. The Kalundborg eco-industrial park in Copenhagen is probably the most well-known example of a successful experiment with redesigning industry on ecological lines. A shift from an emphasis on goods to an emphasis on services is the third interlinking principle of natural capitalism. This change in the business model would result in a better alignment of both the customer's needs and the producer's objectives.

For example, when one leases an elevator service, rather than purchase elevators, the customer benefits as he or she does not have to be responsible for the operation or maintenance and upkeep of the elevator. The service provider benefits from lower operating costs owing to its superior products and a better maintained elevator. Finally, the last principle relates to the reinvestment of profits from business initiatives into creating and maintaining natural capital. Most natural resource-intensive industries, such as fisheries, paper, and forestry, are already doing this, but other industries need to follow suit.

Adapted from http://abc.net.au/science/slab/natcap/

in the premise of capitalism and market-based economies, and instead talks of an entirely new paradigm called radical ecology. This talks of incorporating ecological concerns explicitly into all production and consumption decisions, even if it adversely affects private profitability and violates private property rights. Ecological concerns supersede all other economic and social concerns. We will now turn to these two schools of thought. The next section discusses natural capitalism and the concomitant opportunities and challenges. This is followed by a deliberation on radical ecology, and the challenges that this approach poses for the global economy. We then conclude the chapter with some thoughts about the enabling conditions that would result in sustainable development, regardless of the underlying economic model.

Natural Capitalism

Market-based capitalism, as we know it today, is based on a mind-set that is focused on economic growth through the accumulation of capital, which, in turn, embodies new knowledge and technologies. A capitalist firm has to grow and reduce its costs through increasing the productivity of its resources such as machinery and labor if it is to survive in a competitive environment. This is the only way by which it can earn profits and continue to grow, or else it would be driven out of the market system. It may be noted that that capitalism does not guarantee profits. However, it guarantees and protects the right to private property and its use by the owner. Business firms operate in a market where transactions are voluntary and the price mechanism allocates resources to their best (most productive) uses. There are three implications of this. The first is that any shortage of a particular resource in terms of its availability would induce business firms to search for substitutes and alternatives. This search may be aided by knowledge-creating institutions, such as universities and research laboratories. The second implication is that demand for products and services of firms is driven by utility maximizing households whose changes in tastes and preferences are reflected in the market price mechanism. The final implication is that growth in size and capacity is the key to survival and ultimately, success. When we aggregate over all firms and business organizations, growth in total output is taken to be the most important yardstick of success in (at least potentially), increasing human wellbeing. While the traditional microeconomic theory does develop the concept of an optimal size of a production unit depending on the economics of production, macroeconomics has no such corresponding measure for a nation.

The origins of this view of the world go back centuries. During the past 200 years, there has been a phenomenal growth in material prosperity across the world, and a large body of economic theory has been created based on an implicit assumption that natural capital has little or no value as compared to the value of final production. The standard business model is a linear sequence of extraction, production, and distribution. The use of raw materials is acknowledged as is the disposal of wastes created during the productive process. The conventional view is that, if there is enough money to buy, natural resources will always be available, and in a similar fashion, there will always be a place to dump wastes without incurring costs.

Some writers have (Hawken, Lovins, and Lovins1999) argued that capitalism can be transformed and *corrected* if the environment and natural capital is brought into the decision-making process in an integral manner. Hence, the environment would not be considered as a minor factor of production, but rather an entire system that was essential to the economy. Capitalism must also acknowledge that life-support systems like air, water, fertility of the top soil, and so on have no substitutes, even though they may not have a direct value in the market place. Hence, one way of addressing this integration is to find appropriate ways to assign economic values to all kinds of capital, like manufactured, financial, human, and natural capital. The entire economic system comprising firms and households, as well as markets and policymakers, would have to acknowledge that reduction of economic inequality and enhancing employment opportunities for all would be important necessary conditions to reduce use of material resources, over-consumption, and wastes. In such a system, the needs of people would trump the needs of business with the help of responsive democratic institutions.

The transition to natural capitalism would require some significant changes in how business is conducted and the patterns of production and consumption in a society. Business strategy changes would entail a completely new approach to the use of resources in production. Resource productivity would have to be radically increased so that resource depletion is slowed down at one end of the value chain and pollution is controlled at the other. The yardstick of technological innovation has to be its energy- and resource-saving potential. In this context, business has a lot to learn from natural processes regarding reduction or even elimination of wastes. In nature, there is no waste, in the sense that one ecosystem's waste is another system's productive resource. It is possible for businesses to redesign industrial systems on biological lines, which enable continuous reuse of materials in closed cycles. This is often referred to as biomimicry. Such significant shifts from the business-as-usual model would require a completely new relationship between the producer and the consumer. Many economists (Heinrichs 2013; Princen, Maniates, and Conca 2002) have argued that this new relationship would be a movement away from the sale and purchase of goods to one where the producer would provide a flow of services to the consumer. This, in turn, would entail a new perception of value where quality of the services that would define the standard of living would be more important than the acquisition of material goods as wealth. Finally, natural capitalism would have to devise ways and means of investing heavily in natural capital. These investments would have to help sustain, restore, and even expand stocks of natural capital such that the biosphere can increase its potential to provide ecosystem services. In this context, it is important to note that natural capital should not be viewed as a collection of things, but as an interrelated and integrated *system* that must be viewed as a whole.

Clearly, a transition to such a system of capitalism would require a complete overhauling of both corporate and consumer culture. It has been argued that this transition, if made, would provide new market opportunities, new sources of growth, and employment and new lifestyles. Two things are worth taking note of at this juncture; the first relates to how to bring about the change in mind-set required for this transition. Would it take a long period of time, or is there a need for some natural catastrophe to shock the world into action? The second issue is whether the standard institutions of markets, government policies, and existing systems of property laws will be able to accommodate the new mind-set.

To understand and explain the opportunities provided by natural capitalism, business organizations will have to be more open to solicit support from competitors, consumers, and government, as well as social organizations with which they may have had an adversarial relationship in the past. This might seem an impossible proposition for any profit-making competitive business firm, but many organizations and companies are beginning to do exactly that. Some specialized organizations, such as the Rocky Mountain Institute and the World Resources Institute, consult regularly for business houses and communities. For instance, one of the largest forest product companies of the world is working on a common strategic plan with Rainforest Action Network and Greenpeace, its former arch-enemies (Moffat 2001). Similarly, Mitsubishi has collaborated with 160 non-governmental environmental organizations to create a new vision for the company (Hawken, Lovins, and Lovins 1999, p. 317).

The proponents of natural capitalism are optimistic about the transition for a number of reasons. Firstly, when practical solutions to problems are proposed based on the principle of systems thinking and design, people are ready to change their preferences. Secondly, natural capitalism, as an earth- and environment-friendly alternative to business as usual is already witnessing the emergence of a consensus from many sections of society beyond government and big business. Thirdly, optimism springs from the fact that a large number of independent groups have created common frameworks of understanding the urgency of environmental problems across the world. This, they assert, has never happened in politics, economics, or religion, but is happening as a growing movement toward sustainability (Edwards 2005).

The aforementioned examples and reasons demonstrate that transition may be possible, but given the nature of change, it would take a significant period of time and effort. However, given the immediacy of the impacts of climate change on the global economy, the time dimension is of essence, and there is a deep concern whether, even if all other parameters are enabling, there is enough time to make the transition from capitalism as we know it today, to natural capitalism. Several examples (Gardner, Prugh, and Starke 2008) about applications of natural capitalism in business and real life are offered by its advocates. What is of concern, however, is whether these can be scaled-up and take on a global dimension, or whether they would remain as examples of the art of the possible, a set of case studies, to read and debate about.

Radical Ecology

There is another group of thinkers who have been arguing that private property-based market capitalism would have to be replaced by a new set of institutions, which would reflect a new socioeconomic order of things (Foster 2002, 2009; Williams, 2010). Proponents of this radical ecology assert that the fundamental dynamic of capitalism is to accumulate wealth and increase consumption. It works on the principle of self-interest, and not social considerations. For instance, if we are to leave the world with enough resources for future generations, it may clash with one's own self-interest, related to one's life expectancy. Hence, the time horizon of all self-interested decision-making that is hardwired into the capitalist system would itself be an insurmountable challenge. This is definitely true for households and individuals. As far as businesses are concerned, they might have a planning horizon, which is greater than the life span of an individual and are usually guided by the current situation of competition and demand in the market. In essence, any form of private property, self-interest-based capitalism would usually place a higher value on the present than on the distant future. It has a tendency to create inequalities in outcomes as far as wealth and income are concerned. High levels of inequality would generate tendencies to waste by the rich and overexploitation of the environment by the very poor. Putting it starkly, the philosophy of capitalism does not contain in its vocabulary the word *enough*.

If the society–nature relationship is to be looked at in terms of a systemic whole, which is complex and about which we have incomplete knowledge and understanding, then some form of long-term planning becomes essential for managing the depletion of resources and the creation of wastes. Planning would also be necessary for reducing extreme inequalities that trigger unsustainable use of resources. New ways of treating ecological resources and minimizing wastes could reduce the demand for employment, and systematic planning is required to generate suitable employment opportunities. This planning need not imply large government or big bureaucracy; rather, it would entail a large set of guidelines for resource use and business processes. Further, it would be essential for local communities and businesses to adhere to these guidelines for which appropriate incentive mechanisms must be put in place. The objective of the exercise would be to integrate the constraints posed by natural systems into the decision-making process, along with other economic constraints.

One aspect of economic change brought about by a capitalist system of production and exchange is a continuous reworking of society's relationship with the biophysical world. Human beings continuously build a new kind of nature by transforming natural resources into manufactured goods, buildings, urban spaces, and other physical assets. This process of transformation is carried out through production and exchange in markets, which supposedly reflect society's priorities and preferences. This requires transferable private property rights and rules to enforce them, which would cover the biophysical world such as land and other natural resources. This process of a continuous transformation degrades the natural environment through depletion of resources and creation of wastes. No system that is essentially based on private property can reverse the damage done to nature, whether in the present or in the future. Not only that, markets, in the process of continuously commodifying nature, also create human wastes, that is, human beings who are wasted. The wastage of human lives can come from many sources: for instance, people could be displaced when natural resources are depleted, such as cutting of forests or building of large dams, or they may be displaced as an outcome of technological change seeking a more efficient way to produce, leading to people and their skills becoming redundant resulting in a large unemployed labor force. This is often referred to, in the radical ecology literature, as accumulation though dispossession, where a few people acquire wealth by dispossessing others, rather than creating new wealth.

The classical Marxist critique of capitalism was built around the inherent instability of capitalist production systems and the consequent struggle between capitalists and workers as two distinct classes. Marx and Engels (Engels 1908; Marx 1959/1844; Parsons 1977) were aware that capitalism necessarily despoils nature, but focused on the primary social conflict between two classes of people. Radical ecologists (Jones 2011) point out that, in the current stage of capitalist development, the primary contradiction lies in the relationship of capitalism's logic of change and nature's own rules of the biophysical world. The radical ecologists, therefore, believe that it is unlikely that capitalism can be reformed to deal with its relationship with the natural world such that a more harmonious evolution could take place. This is particularly so because congruence with nature requires a different type of property system, which would be governed by a complex and multi-layered system of usufruct rights, customs, and obligations, where nature would be looked at as shared common property. This sharing would have to be understood not only as one among human beings, but among all other living beings too.

As ecological constraints become binding and come in the way for further economic development, the only way to address this challenge is by dismantling the system of private property rights and bring in common property rights or leased property rights, where the decision-making authority shifts from the self-interested individual to a collective of people who have broader ecological interests and a sense of stewardship of nature so as to ensure long-term sustainability. Thus, capitalism would have to be turned on its head, as institutional wisdom would guide and direct economic decision-making.

The role of developing appropriate institutions to spearhead such a radical change is underscored. Representative organizations at the global level that can comprehend the enormity of the ecological challenge and match it with economic needs and aspirations are required. We would also need local institutions that could interpret the broad guidelines of the umbrella organizations and implement them. Community action would be required both locally to implement change and globally, where experience and scientific knowledge must be blended. Further, as engines for implementation, business mind-sets must adapt to the new concepts of leased or common property rights, and yet contribute to serving economic needs through innovations and appropriate management practices. The details of this set of changes are difficult to predict, but the objective would be to create a new economic order where ecological concerns would be given priority over anthropogenic needs, and would drive all production and consumption decisions.

If one has to argue that capitalism cannot be reformed enough to define a sustainable relationship with nature, then new institutions and property relations would have to be defined and created. Such radical social changes would not come about without opposition from certain sections of business that stand to gain by utilizing nature for private profit. Some Marxist's (Gramsci 1971) have argued that the state and the capitalist class, even in the face of economic crisis, can control and mitigate opposition from the working class. This is typically done, partly through coercion and use of force, and partly through a more subtle creation of consent, for the prevalent order of things. In the case of the contradiction of capitalism's inherent logic of accumulation with the degradation and depletion of nature, there is no way that consent can be manufactured in nature. If the relationship with nature becomes essentially one of coercion, then, as is becoming increasingly obvious to scientists, nature can be quite cruel in its reaction and retaliation. Indeed, human beings living in society are not fully aware of the kind of severity with which nature might hit back. The crux of this argument is that there are no feedback and automatic corrective mechanisms in the capital–nature relationship unlike the capital-labor contradiction.

A question could then arise that if left to itself, capital is unlikely to radically alter its relationship with nature, would the arising crisis jeopardize all life on earth. There would be no possibility of creating a new social order as a revolutionary outcome. Therefore, social movements that transcend the standard working class struggles need to incessantly question the business-as-usual model and its impact on the environment. These movements must also imagine alternative ways of managing and sharing nature's resources and creating a sustainable relationship with both the biotic and abiotic parts of the environment. It will require imagining and practicing new lifestyles and benchmarking new technologies in terms of reduced material and energy intensities. Finally, these movements must nurture an understanding of the intrinsic value of nature and the impact of deciding on new products and production systems on future generations.

Concluding Thoughts

In this chapter, we have argued that the system of global market capitalism would have to undergo major changes if sustainable development is to become a reality. In this context, two radical strands of thought have been briefly discussed. The first strand focuses on the possibility of reforming capitalism to integrate ecological considerations in every aspect of decision-making. The core argument demonstrates that this natural capitalism is consistent with markets, individual incentives, and private property. The state would have to play a more proactive role, acting as an intermediary between local and global institutions that regulate environmental issues. The second strand argues that no form of capitalism based on individual incentives and private property can completely alter the system's relationship with nature. Hence, this second strand's core argument revolves around the need to transform individual incentives and private property into more collective property and shared prosperity. This approach would call for more radical social movements to challenge some of the fundamental institutions of capitalism. The role of the state would be even more critical as it shapes new mind-sets and new approaches by redefining the basic tenets of capitalism such as property rights. Its role would be way beyond just regulation and oversight.

A welcome sign of change toward sustainability over the past three or four decades has been that both the aforementioned aspects of transformation to a new economic order are discernible. On the one hand, new rules and regulations, new technologies, and new business models have, in many activities, been able to reduce the adverse impact of economic development on the environment. Often, businesses have formally taken the initiative to voluntarily reduce wastes and become more eco-efficient. On the other hand, there are many community initiatives and citizen's movements that have been gathering support for change toward sustainability, as well as experimenting with new lifestyles (See Box 12.2).

Box 12.2 Ecological movements: Hopeful signs for a sustainability revolution

Curitiba: A Model City

Curitiba is a city of more than two million people in southern Brazil. Often referred to as the greenest city on earth, it has over 50 sq. m of green space per capita. Small parks in the city are filled with shrines to different cultures of the world. There is a world-class botanical garden and an opera house built on an abandoned quarry with its glass walls shimmering with the reflection of the water. The cities' bus rapid transit system (BRTS) covers about 80 percent of the daily transportation needs of its residents. The park system, sewage management systems, and storm management facilities are planned to be serving well-defined ecological functions.

The city is not a newly built one, but a space that was transformed by conscious comprehensive urban planning. It is still an industrial city with many large automobile and industrial firms producing there. The transformation of this city is essentially due to the architect and urban planner Jamie Lerner, who was also a three-time mayor of Curitiba. The change toward sustainability was not due to a grassroots movement, but was led by the vision of the mayor and his team of experts and professionals who designed a new Curitiba in comprehensive detail. The mayor's projects and programs never faced resistance, partly due to the presence of the military government that ruled Brazil from 1964 to 1985, when electoral politics was not allowed. Curitiba, like other cities of Brazil, was also known for its favelas, which are unplanned slums inhabited by disenfranchised people, often migrants from rural areas. People living in the favelas have been brought under a program where trash and recyclables are exchanged for bus tokens, food, and cash. Because of this, the city is astonishingly clean, and the efforts of these people have been greatly appreciated by the general populace.

This is a story where comprehensive planning was effectively implemented without having to deal with the complications of electoral politics toward building a sustainable city.

Sources: https://theguardian.com/cities/2016/may/06/story-of-cities-37-mayor-jaime-lerner-curitiba-brazil-green-capital-global-icon
https://en.wikipedia.org/wiki/Curitiba
http://abc.net.au/science/slab/natcap/

The Silent Valley Movement

The Silent Valley Movement in India's southern state of Kerala is a remarkable story of a spontaneous grassroots people's movement that saved a pristine evergreen forest from being destroyed by a hydroelectric project. In the mid-1970s, the state government of Kerala decided to take up a project to install four units of hydroelectric power stations of 60 MWs each. This would provide critically needed additional power to the residents, irrigate an additional 100 sq.km and provide employment to several thousand people.

This project was taken up despite a number of reports by environmentalists, activists, as well as the National Committee on Environment Planning and Coordination (NCEPC). All recommended the project be scrapped because it would destroy biodiversity, cause illegal felling, poaching, and encroachments, all of which would ultimately destroy the valley. The NCEPC's recommendation had a loophole, however. It suggested that, if abandoning the project was not possible, a set of safeguards should be implemented. The state government took advantage of the loophole and also claimed that the assessment of potential damage was overestimated.

The work of some activists and conservationists fortunately found a lot of support from the general assembly of the International Union for the Conservation of Nature. Some NGOs, the local media (which had originally supported the construction of the power plant), and above all, the local populace took up the cause of opposing the project. The central government in New Delhi continued to be in favor of the project.

In 1981, when a new Prime Minister was elected at the center who took personal interest in environmental conservation, there was an increase of pressure exerted by the people's movement on the central government. In 1983, the power project was called off, and in 1985, the valley around which the protests were centered was declared as Silent Valley National Park, which is now a popular tourist destination.

Sources: http://conservationindia.org/case-studies/silent-valley-a-peoples-movement-that-saved-a-foresthttps://en.wikipedia.org/wiki/Save_Silent_Valley

The good news about both these strands of change toward sustainability is that there are overlaps and commonalities that can create a collective pressure. Both call for a change in values regarding the importance of nature and sustaining the human–nature relationship with a better appreciation of the place of the human species in the bigger frame of the biophysical world. The second shared feature is that, in both the strands of thought, there is a dawning awareness that the way we evaluate new technologies would have to change. They would have to be benchmarked, not against convenience or costs, but against their efficiency in energy and material use. Finally, there is a common awareness that, with ecological considerations, getting primacy and features of new technology altering sharply, products and the way they are consumed would be subject to change. Hence, it would require not only a change in mind-sets, but also actual lifestyles and consumption patterns. For each of these enablers, there is a collective feature that runs through, which is going beyond a myopic self-interest to a more enlightened one, where individual advantage is balanced against a concern for all living things, including those yet unborn.

References

Agrawal, A., and M.C. Lemos. 2007. "A Greener Revolution in the Making?: Environmental Governance in the 21st Century." *Environment: Science and Policy for Sustainable Development* 49, no. 5, pp. 36–45.

Arrow K.J. 1963. *Social Choice and Individual Values.* 2nd ed. New York: Wiley.

Arrow, K., B. Bolin, R. Costanza, P. Dasgupta, C. Folke, C.S. Holling, B.O. Jansson, S. Levin, K.G. Maler, C. Perrings, and D. Pimentel. 1996. "Economic Growth, Carrying Capacity, and the Environment." *Ecological Applications* 6, no. 1, pp. 13–15. doi:10.2307/2269539

Arrow, K.J. 1950. "A Difficulty in the Concept of Social Welfare." *Journal of Political Economy* 58, no. 4, pp. 328–46. doi:10.1086/256963

Arrow,K.P., L. Dasgupta, G. Goulder, P. Daily, G. Ehrlich, S. Heal, K.G. Levin, K. Mäler, S. Schneider, D. Starrett, and B. Walker. 2004. "Are We Consuming Too Much." Journal of Economic Perspectives 18, no. 3, pp. 147–72.

Basu K., P. Pattanaik, and K. Suzumara (eds). 1995. Choice, Welfare and Freedom: A Fetschrift in Honour of Amartya K Sen. Oxford, UK: Clarendon Press.

Beder, S. 2002. "Putting the Boot In." *The Ecologist* 32, no. 3, pp. 24–28, 66–7.

Bentham, J. 1907. "An Introduction to the Principles of Morals and Legislation." *Library of Economics and Liberty*. Retrieved May 16, 2017 from http://econlib.org/library/Bentham/bnthPML.html

Bergson, A. 1938. "A Reformulation of Certain Aspects of Welfare Economics." *Quarterly Journal of Economics* 52, no. 2, pp. 310–34.

Bolt, K., M. Matete, and M. Clemens. 2002. "Manual for Calculating Adjusted Net Savings Environment Department." World Bank. Retrieved from https://siteresources.worldbank.org/INTEEI/1105643115814965717/20486606/Savingsmanual2002.pdf

Borda, J.C. 1781. *Mémoire sur les élections au scrutin.* Histoire de l'Académie Royale des Sciences. Paris.

Boulding, K.E. 1966. "The Economics of the Coming Spaceship Earth." In *Environmental Quality in a Growing Economy*, ed. H. Jarrett, 3–14. Baltimore, MD: Resources for the Future/Johns Hopkins University Press.

Butler, C. 2002. *Postmodernism: A Very Short Introduction.* New York: Oxford University Press.

Chamberlin, E.H. 1933. *The Theory of Monopolistic Competition.* Cambridge, MA: Harvard University Press.

Chambers, D., and J.T. Guo. 2009. "Natural Resources and Economic Growth: Some Theory and Evidence." *Annals of Economics and Finance* 10, no. 2, pp. 367–89.

Chester, L. 2013. "To Change or Reform Capitalism." *Review of Radical Political Economic*s 46, no. 3, pp. 406–12.

Coase, R. 1960. "The Problem of Social Cost." Journal of Law and Economics 3, no. 1, pp. 1–44. doi:10.1086/466560

Cohen, J. 1997. "Population, Economics, Environment and Culture: An Introduction to Human Carrying Capacity." *Journal of Applied Ecology* 34, pp. 1325–33.

Common, M., and S. Stagl. 2005. *E* Weisel *cological Economics: An Introduction.* Cambridge: University Press.

Condorcet, M.D. 1785. *Essai sur l'application de l'analyse a la probabilitk des dkcisions rendues d la probabilith des voix.* Paris: De l'imprimerie royale.

Corell, R. 2007. quoted in Guardian 14 September 2007. Greenland is Now a Country Fit for Broccoli Growers Retrieved from https://theguardian.com/commentisfree/2007/sep/14/comment.climatechange

Costanza, R. (ed). 1991. *Ecological Economics: The Science and Management of Sustainability.* New York: Columbia University Press.

Costanza, R., and H.E. Daly. 1987. "Toward an Ecological Economics." *Ecol. Modelling* 38, pp. 1–7.

Daly, H.E. 1991. *Steady-State Economics.* Washington: Island Press.

Daly, H.E. 1996. *Beyond Growth: The Economics of Sustainable Development.* Boston: Beacon Press. ISBN 9780807047095.

Daly, H.E., and R.J.A. Goodland. 1998. "Imperatives for Environmental Sustainability: Decrease Overconsumption and Stabilize Population." In *Population and Global Security*, ed. N. Polunin. Cambridge: Cambridge University Press.

Dasgupta, P. 1993. *An Inquiry into Well-Being and Destitution.* Oxford: Clarendon Press.

Dasgupta, P. 2001. *Human Wellbeing and the Natural Environment.* New Delhi: Oxford University Press.

Dasgupta, P. 2010. "The Place of Nature in Economic Development, Chapter 74." In Handbook of Development Economics, 5, 4977–5046. Amsterdam: North Holland.

Dasgupta, P., and G. Heal. 1979. *Economic Theory and Exhaustible Resources.* Cambridge: Cambridge University Press.

Dasgupta. P. 2009. "The Welfare Economic Theory of Green National Accounts." *Environmental and Resource Economics* 42, no. 1, pp. 3–38. doi:10.1007/s10640-008-9223-y

Deaton, A. 2013. *The Great Escape: Health, Wealth, and the Origins of Inequality.* Princeton: Princeton University Press.

Edgeworth, F.Y. 1881. *Mathematical Psychics: An Essay on the Application of Mathematics to the Moral Sciences*. London: Kegan Paul & Co.

Edwards, A.R. 2005. *The Sustainability Revolution: Portrait of a Paradigm Shift*. Gabriola Island, Canada: New Society Publishers.

Ehrlich, P.R. 1968. *The Population Bomb*. New York: Ballantine.

Eisner, M.A. 2004. "Corporate Environmentalism, Regulatory Reform and Industry Self-Regulation: Toward Genuine Regulatory Reinvention in the United States." *Governance: An International Journal of Policy, Administration and Institutions* 17, no. 2, pp. 145–67.

Elizabeth, K. 2006. *Field Notes from a Catastrophe, Man Nature and Climate Change*. New York: Bloomsbury.

Engels, F. 1908. *Socialism: Utopian and Scientific*. Chicago: Charles H Kerr and Co.

Engels, F. 1940. *Dialectics of Nature*. Moscow: Progress Publishers.

Esty, D.C., M. Levy, T. Srebotnjak, and A. De Sherbinin. 2005. *Environmental Sustainability Index: Benchmarking National Environmental Stewardship*. New Haven: Yale Center for Environmental Law and Policy.

Finkmoore, R.J. 2010. *Environmental Law and Values of Nature*. Durham: Carolina Academic Press.

Forrester, J.W. 1971. *World Dynamics*. Waltham, Massachusetts: Pegasus Communications.

Foster, B.J. 2002. *Ecology Against Capitalism*. New York: Monthly Review Press.

Foster, B.J. 2009. *The Ecological Revolution: Making Peace with the Planet*. New York: Monthly Review Press.

Funtowicz, S., and J. Ravetz. 2003. "Post-Normal Science." *Internet Encyclopaedia of Ecological Economics*, International Society for Ecological Economics retrieved from http://isecoeco.org/pdf/pstnormsc.pdf

Furtado. C. 1964. *Development and Under-development*, 52–56, 59–60, 72, 115–116. Berkeley: University of California Press.

Gardner, G.T., T. Prugh, and L. Starke. 2008. *State of the World 2008: Innovations for a Sustainable Economy: A Worldwatch Institute Report On Progress Toward a Sustainable Society*. New York: W.W. Norton.

Gramsci, A. 1971. *Selections from the Prison Notebooks*. New York: International Publishers.

Harrod, R. 1939. "An Essay in Dynamic Theory." *Economic Journal* 49, pp. 14–33.

Hawken, P., A. Lovins, L.H. Lovins. 1999. *Natural Capitalism: Creating the Next Industrial Revolution*. Boston: Little, Brown.

Heinrichs, H. 2013. "Sharing Economy: A Potential New Pathway to Sustainability." *Gaia* 22, no. 4, pp. 228–31. Retrieved from https://search.proquest.com/docview/1471962034?accountid=42623

Hicks, J.R. 1939. "The Foundations of Welfare Economics." *The Economic Journal* 49, no. 196, pp. 696–712. 10.2307/2225023

Hirschman, A.O. 1969. "The Strategy of Economic Development." In *Accelerating Investment in Developing Economies,* eds. A.N. Agarwal and S.P. Singh. London: Oxford Press.

Hotelling, H. 1931. "The Economics of Exhaustible Resources." *J. Pol. Econ.* 39, pp. 137–75.

http://ecologicalfootprint.com/

http://footprint.wwf.org.uk/

IPCC 2014. *Climate Change 2014: Synthesis Report.* Contribution of Working Groups I, II and III to the Fifth Assessment Report of the Intergovernmental Panel on Climate Change [Core Writing Team, R.K. Pachauri and L.A. Meyer (eds.)]. IPCC, Geneva, Switzerland, p. 151.

Jevons, W.S.1906. *The Coal Question: An Inquiry Concerning the Progress of the Nation, and the Probable Exhaustion of Our Coal-Mines,* 3rd ed., rev. London: Macmillan. (Original work published 1865).

Jones, A.W. 2011. "Solving the Ecological Problems of Capitalism: Capitalist and Socialist Possibilities." *Organization & Environment* 24, no. 1, pp. 54–73.

Jones, C.I., and D. Vollrath. 2013. *Introduction to Economic Growth.* New York, London: W. W Norton Inc.

Kaldor, N. 1939. "Welfare Propositions of Economics and Interpersonal Comparisons of Utility." *The Economic Journal* 49, no. 195, pp. 549–552. 10.2307/2224835

Keynes, J.M. 1936. *The General Theory of Employment, Interest and Money.* London: Macmillan and Co, Ltd.

Kolbert, E. 2015. *The Sixth Extinction an Unnatural History.* London: Bloomsbury.

Kolstad, C.D. 2000. *Environmental Economics.* New York and Oxford: Oxford University Press.

Koopmans, T.C. 1960. "Stationary Ordinal Utility and Impatience." *Econometrica* 28, pp. 287–309.

Koopmans, T.C. 1965. "On the Concept of Optimal Economic Growth." In *The Economic Approach to Development Planning*, 225–87. Chicago: Rand McNally.

Krausmann, F., K.H. Erb, S. Gingrich, H. Haberl, A. Bondeau, V. Gaube, C. Lauk, C. Plutzar, and T.D. Searchinger. 2013. "Global Human Appropriation of Net Primary Production Doubled in the 20th Century." Proceedings of the National Academy of Sciences of the United States of America 110, no. 25, pp. 10324–29.

Lewis, W.A. 1954. "Economic Development with Unlimited Supplies of Labour." *The Manchester School* 22, pp. 139–91. doi:10.1111/j.1467-9957.1954. tb00021.x

Little, I.M.D., and J.A. Mirrlees. 1969. *Manual of Industrial Project Analysis,* Vol. II. Paris: OECD Development Centre.

Malthus, T.R. 1826. *An Essay on the Principle of Population.* Library of Economics and Liberty. Retrieved June 23, 2017 from http://econlib.org/library/Malthus/malPlong1.html

Marshall, A. 1920. *Principles of Economics.* Library of Economics and Liberty. Retrieved June 23, 2017 from http://econlib.org/library/Marshall/marP.html

Marx, K. 1959/1844. *Economic and Philosophical Manuscripts of 1844.* Moscow: Progress Publishers.

Marx, K. 1981. *Capital: The Process of Capital Production as a Whole,* Vol III. Harmondsworth Penguin. Translated by David Fernbach. Edited by Frederick Engels.

McLellan, R (editor in chief). 2014. Living Planet Report 2014. World Wildlife Fund.

Meadows, D., D. Meadows, J. Randers, and W. Behrens. 1972. *The Limits to Growth: A Report for the Club of Rome on the Predicament of Mankind.* New York: Universe Books.

Meyer, L.H. 2003. "Past and Future: The Case for a Threshold Notion of Harm." In *Rights, Culture and the Law: Themes from the Legal and Political Philosophy of Joseph Raz,* eds. L.H. Meyer, S.L. Paulson, and T.W. Pogge. Oxford: Oxford University Press.

Milberg, W. 1988. "The Language of Economics: Deconstructing the Neoclassical Text." *Social Concept* 4, pp. 33–57.

Mill, J.S. 1909. *Principles of Political Economy with some of their Applications to Social Philosophy,* ed. W.J. Ashley. Library of Economics and Liberty. Retrieved from http://econlib.org/library/Mill/mlP.html

Mill, J.S., J. Bentham, and A. Ryan. 1987. *Utilitarianism and Other Essays.* Harmondsworth, Middlesex, England: Penguin Books.

Miller, G.T., Jr. 1971. *Energetics, Kinetics, and Life: An Ecological Approach*, 293. Wadsworth Pub. Co.

Moffat, J. 2001. *Victory for the Forests: Greenpeace's Market Campaign for the Great Bear Rainforest,* p. 91. Learning & Innovations Institute, Coady International Institute. Retrieved from http://coady.stfx.ca/tinroom/assets/file/Jeanne%20Moffat.pdf

Najam, A., M. Papa, and N. Taiyab. 2006. *Global Environmental Governance a Reform Agenda.* Denmark: International Institution for Sustainable Development.

Nelson, R.R. 1956. "A Theory of the Low Level Equilibrium Trap." *American Economic Review* 46, pp. 894–908.

Neumayer, E. 2000. "Scarce or Abundant? The Economics of Natural Resource Availability." *Journal of Economic Surveys* 14, no. 3, pp. 185–92.

Neumayer, E. 2003. *Weak versus Strong Sustainability: Exploring the Limits of Two Opposing Paradigms.* Northampton, MA: Edward Elgar.

Newman, J. (ed). 2011. *Green Ethics and Philosophy: An A-to-Z Guide.* Los Angeles, CA: Sage Publications.

Nozick, R. 1974. *Anarchy, State, and Utopia.* New York: Basic Books.

Nurkse, R. 1961. Problems of Capital Formation in Underdeveloped Countries, 163. New York: Oxford University Press.

Osberg, L., and A. Sharpe. 2002. "An Index of Economic Well-Being for Selected OECD Countries." *The Review of Income and Wealth* 48, no. 3, September, pp. 291–316.

Pareto, V. 1971 [1906]. *Manual of Political Economy.* New York: A.M. Kelley.

Parsons, H L. (ed). 1977. *Marx and Engels on Ecology,* Westport, Connecticut: Greenwood Press.

Passmore, J. 1980. *Man's Responsibility for Nature: Ecological Problems and Western Traditions,* 2nd ed. (corrected, with new pref. and appendix). Duckworth: London [England].

Pearce, D.W., K. Hamilton, and G. Atkinson. 1996. "Measuring Sustainable Development: Progress on Indicators." *Environment and Development Economics* 1, no. 1, pp. 85–101.

Pezzey, J.V., and M.A. Toman. 2002. *The Economics of Sustainability: A Review of Journal Articles,* Discussion Paper 02-03, Washington DC: Resources for the Future.

Pigou, A.C. 1964. *The Economics of Welfare.* London: McMillan.

Piketty, T., and A. Goldhammer. 2014. *Capital in the Twenty-first Century.* Cambridge, Massachusetts: The Belknap Press of Harvard University Press.

Piketty, T., and A. Goldhammer. 2015. *The Economics of Inequality.* Cambridge, Massachusetts: The Belknap Press of Harvard University Press.

Pletcher, G.K. 1981. "The Rights of Future Generations." In *Responsibilities to Future Generations,* ed. E. Partridge. New York: Prometheus Books.

Prebisch, R. 1970. Transformation and Development. Washington, DC: American Development Bank Survey.

Princen, T., M. Maniates, and K. Conca. 2002. *Confronting Consumption.* Cambridge: MIT Press.

Ramsey. F.P. 1928. "A Mathematical Theory of Savings." Economic Journal 38, no. 12, pp. 543–59.

Rawls, J. 1971. *A Theory of Justice.* Cambridge, Massachusetts: Harvard University Press.

Ricardo, D. 1966. *The Works and Correspondence of David Ricardo, Volume I on the Principles of Political Economy and Taxation,* ed. P. Sraffa. Cambridge University Press.

Robbins, L. 1935. *An Essay on the Nature and Significance of Economic Science,* 2nd ed. London: Macmillan.

Robinson, J. 1933. *The Economics of Imperfect Competition.* London: Macmillan and Co., Ltd.

Romer, P.M. 1994. "The Origins of Endogenous Growth." *The Journal of Economic Perspectives* 8, no. 1, pp. 3–22. doi:10.1257/jep.8.1.3. JSTOR 2138148.

Rosenstein-Rodan, P.N. 1943. "Problems of Industrialisation of Eastern and South-Eastern Europe." *The Economic Journal* 53, no. 210/211, pp. 202–11. doi:10.2307/2226317

Rostow, W.W. 1960. *The Stages of Economic Growth: A Non-Communist Manifesto.* Cambridge University Press.

Samuelson, P. 1956. "Social Indifference Curves." *Quarterly Journal of Economics* 70, no. 1, pp. 1–22.

Samuelson, P.A. 1961. "The Evaluation of 'Social Income': Capital Formation and Wealth." In *The Theory of Capital,* eds. F.A. Lutz and D.C. Hague. London: MacMillan.

Sarkar, R. 2017. *Business Institutions Environment.* New Delhi, India: Oxford University Press.

Sen, A. 1973. *On Economic Inequality.* Oxford: Clarendon Press.

Sen, A. 1984. *Resources, Values and Development.* Oxford: Basil Blackwell.

Sen, A. 1987. *On Ethics and Economics.* Oxford and New York: Basil Blackwell.

Sen, A. 2001. *Development as Freedom.* Oxford, New York: Oxford University Press.

Sen, A. 2002. *Rationality and Freedom.* New Delhi, India: Oxford University Press.

Sen, A. 2017. *Collective Choice and Social Welfare.* Cambridge, MA: Harvard University Press.

Sen, A., and B. Williams (ed). 1982. *Utilitarianism and Beyond.* Cambridge: Cambridge University Press.

Sinha, A. 2004. "Living to Consume and Consuming to Live." In *Business Social Partnerships—The International Perspective,* ed. S. Singh Sengupta. Jaipur: Aalekh Publishers.

Smith, A. 1776/1976. *An Inquiry into the Nature and Causes of the Wealth of Nations.* Oxford: Clarendon Press.

Solow, R. 1993. "An Almost Practical Step Toward Sustainability." *Resources Policy* 19, no. 3, pp. 162–72. Retrieved from http://EconPapers.repec.org/RePEc:eee:jrpoli:v:19:y:1993:i:3:p:162-172

Solow, R.M. 1956. "A Contribution to the Theory of Economic Growth." *Quarterly Journal of Economics* 70, no. 1, pp. 65–94. doi:10.2307/1884513. JSTOR 1884513. Pdf

Solow, R.M. June 1991. "Sustainability: An Economist's Perspective." *18th J. Seward Johnson Lecture,* Marine Policy Center, Woods Hole Oceanographic Institution. Retrieved from http://cda.mrs.umn.edu/~kildegac/Courses/Enviro/3008/Readings/Solow.pdf

Steffen, W., K. Richardson, J. Rockström, S.E. Cornell, I. Fetzer, E.M. Bennett, R. Biggs, S.R. Carpenter, W. de Vries, C.A. de Wit, and C. Folke. 2015.

"Planetary Boundaries: Guiding Human Development on a Changing Planet." *Science* 347, no. 6223, p. 1259855.

Stern, N. 2006. *Stern Review on the Economics of Climate Change*. London, UK: Her Majesty's Treasury.

Stern, N. 2008. "The Economics of Climate Change." *American Economic Review* 98, no. 2, pp. 1–37. doi:10.1257/aer.98.2.1

Stiglitz, J.E. 2012. *The Price of Inequality: How Today's Divided Society Endangers Our Future*. New York: W.W. Norton & Co.

Stiglitz, J.E., A. Sen, and J.P. Fitoussi. 2009. *Report by the Commission on the Measurement of Economic Performance and Social Progress*, p. 291. Retrieved from http://stiglitz-sen-fitoussi.fr/en/index.htm

Stockholm Resilience Centre. 2017. *Planetary Boundaries—an Update*. Retrieved from http://stockholmresilience.org/research/research-news/2015-01-15-planetary-boundaries---an-update.html

Suzumura, K. 1983. *Rational Choice, Collective Decisions, and Social Welfare*. Cambridge Cambridgeshire, New York: Cambridge University Press.

Szekely, F., and H. Strebel. 2012 "Strategic Innovation For Sustainability." *IMD Global Center for Sustainability Leadership. Retrieved from* http://imd.org/research/challenges/strategic-innovation-sustainability-francisco-szekely-heidi-strebel.cfm

Toman, M. 2014. The Need for Multiple Types of Information to Inform Climate Change Assessment. Policy Research Working Paper Series *7094*. The World Bank.

UNECE/Eurostat/OECD 2013. *Framework And Suggested Indicators To Measure Sustainable Development*. Prepared by the Joint UNECE/Eurostat/OECD Task Force on Measuring Sustainable Development. Geneva: UN Economic Commission for Europe. Retrieved from https://unece.org/fileadmin/DAM/stats/documents/ece/ces/2013/SD_framework_and_indicators_final.pdf

United Nations Industrial Development Organization (UNIDO). 1972. *Guidelines for Project Evaluation*. Prepared by P.S. Dasgupta, S.A. Marglin and A.K. Sen. New York: United Nations.

United Nations. 2017. *Sustainable Development Goals: 17 Goals to Transform our World*. Retrieved from http://un.org/sustainabledevelopment/sustainable-development-goals/

Wackernagel, M., and W. Rees. 1995. *Our Ecological Footprint: Reducing Human Impact on the Earth*. Gabriola Island, BC, and Philadelphia, PA: New Society Publishers.

Walras, L. 2013/1874. *Éléments d'économie politique pure, ou théorie de la richesse sociale (Elements of Pure Economics, or the theory of social wealth)*. Routledge: London and New York.

Weisel, G.J. 2013. "Skeptics, Naysayers, Anomalies, and Controversies." In *Climate Change: An Encyclopedia of Science and History ABC-CLIO,* eds. B.C. Black et al., p. 1241.

Weitzman, M.L. 1976. "On the Welfare Significance of National Product in a Dynamic Economy." *Quarterly Journal of Economics* 90, no. 1, pp. 156–62.

Williams, C. 2010. *Ecology and Socialism: Solutions to Capitalist Ecological Crisis.* Chicago: Haymarket Books.

World Commission on Environment and Development. 1987. *Our Common Future.* Oxford: Oxford University Press.

About the Authors

Runa Sarkar is a Professor with the Economics Group at the Indian Institute of Management Calcutta and a member of the committee for the Centre for Development and Environment Policy. Prior to this, she taught at IIT Kanpur. A chemical engineer from BITS Pilani, Runa pursued her Masters in environmental engineering at the University of North Carolina at Chapel Hill, USA. After spending five years as an environmental consultant in a subsidiary of Tata Steel, Runa completed her doctoral studies from IIM Calcutta.

Her interests lie in sustainable development where business interests are in consonance with environmental and social interests. Runa has a penchant for multidisciplinary research and has also been involved in the application of social informatics in the agricultural domain. She has been working in the field of corporate environmental behavior for over two decades, and has published widely in this area. She is the chairperson of CTran Consulting Services, a leading climate change consulting business in India and on the board of the Basix Social Enterprise Group and Basix Consulting and Technology Services. Runa has been a sustainability assessor for CII.

Prof. Sarkar has been one of the co-editors of the India Infrastructure Report (IIR) 2010 on Infrastructure Development in a Low Carbon Economy and IIR 2009 on Land—A Critical Resource for Infrastructure, published by the 3i network. She, along with Prof. Anup Sinha of IIM Calcutta, is the co-author of a book titled Another Development: Participation, Empowerment and Well-being, published by Routledge in early 2015. Another book, titled Environment, Business, Institutions was published by Oxford in April 2017. This is followed by an edited book (jointly edited with Prof. Annapurna Shaw) on Sustainability published by Springer in June 2017.

Anup Sinha is a retired Professor of Economics from the Indian Institute of Management Calcutta where he taught for more than 25 years. He was educated at Presidency College and University of Rochester. He did his doctoral work at the University of Southern California. He has taught at the Centre for Economic Studies, Presidency College and held visiting appointments in a number of institutions in India and abroad such as Indian Institute of Statistics Calcutta, University of Southern California, Washington University at St. Louis, Curtin University of Technology, Perth and Kyoto University. His academic interests and publications are in the areas of sustainable development, ethics, and macroeconomics. He is a former Dean of IIM Calcutta. He has also served as a non-executive Director on the Board of India's National Bank for Agricultural and Rural Development (NABARD). He is also currently serving on the executive committee of the Life Insurance Council of India as the insurance regulator's nominee

He is a popular teacher having won 'Best Teacher' awards from alumni and students of IIM Calcutta. He is a co-author (with Runa Sarkar) of Another Development: Well-Being, Empowerment and Participation in Rural India, Routledge Taylor and Francis 2015. He has co-edited a volume titled Sustainable Development: the Indian Dynamics in 2003. He is currently the Director of Heritage Business School, Kolkata.

Index

OTHER TITLES FROM THE ECONOMICS COLLECTION

Philip Romero, The University of Oregon and
Jeffrey Edwards, North Carolina A&T State University, Editors

- *How the Information Revolution Remade Business and the Economy: A Roadmap for Progress of the Semiconductor Industry* by Apek Mulay
- *Money and Banking: An Intermediate Market-Based Approach, Second Edition* by William D. Gerdes
- *Basic Cost Benefit Analysis for Assessing Local Public Projects, Second Edition* by Barry P. Keating and Maryann O. Keating
- *International Economics, Second Edition: Understanding the Forces of Globalization for Managers* by Paul Torelli
- *The Commonwealth of Independent States Economies: Perspectives and Challenges* by Marcus Goncalves and Erika Cornelius Smith

Announcing the Business Expert Press Digital Library

Concise e-books business students need for classroom and research

This book can also be purchased in an e-book collection by your library as

- a one-time purchase,
- that is owned forever,
- allows for simultaneous readers,
- has no restrictions on printing, and
- can be downloaded as PDFs from within the library community.

Our digital library collections are a great solution to beat the rising cost of textbooks. E-books can be loaded into their course management systems or onto students' e-book readers.
The **Business Expert Press** digital libraries are very affordable, with no obligation to buy in future years. For more information, please visit **www.businessexpertpress.com/librarians**. To set up a trial in the United States, please email **sales@businessexpertpress.com**.